The Consciousness of Joyce

The
Consciousness
of Joyce

RICHARD ELLMANN

OXFORD UNIVERSITY PRESS
Toronto and New York
1977

to Nelly Joyce

Contents

Preface   *page* ix

Introduction   1

Chapter I Homer
1 What's in a Name   10
2 From Daedalus to Dedalus   14
3 Ogygia   19
4 Ulysses' Last Voyage   29
5 Ulysses Redivivus   39

Chapter II Shakespeare
1 Unnatural Murder   45
2 Two Ghosts in *Hamlet*   52
3 Some Versions of Hamlet   59
4 Spacetime   65
5 Cerebral Mating   68

Chapter III Joyce
1 Aesthetics without Aesthetes   73
2 Guerrilla Warfare   77
3 Political Antecedents   82
4 Beyond Parnell   86
5 The Politics of Aesthetics   90

Appendix Joyce's Library in 1920   97

Notes   135

Index   143

Preface

In an earlier book, *Ulysses on the Liffey*, I traced the intricacies of the intellectual patterning which pervades *Ulysses*. Here I try to measure Joyce's response to his principal sources, to show how he reconciled the seemingly irreconcilable, how he unravelled and wove, and how he made his book express his aesthetics and his politics as well as his epic theme.

My work has been made easier by the library of over six hundred books and pamphlets which Joyce had formed by the time he left Trieste for good in 1920. As always, his tenacious brother Stanislaus preserved what James abandoned, and Stanislaus's widow, Mrs. Nelly Joyce, and their son James, have kept them intact and have kindly put them at my disposal. An Appendix to this book lists the collection in full.

In an earlier form the material here was the basis of the Alexander Lectures which I had the honour of giving at the University of Toronto in March 1974. I am grateful to my hospitable hosts there.

Robert O'Clair, J. B. Hainsworth, John V. Kelleher, Mary T. Reynolds, Patrick Henchy, and Ellsworth G. Mason have assisted me with various issues. Mary Ellmann pointed up several problems. I thank Catharine Carver for her careful editing.

In the dedication I acknowledge an old and always increasing debt of gratitude.

R.E.

New College, Oxford
25 October 1976

Introduction

'Consciousness' denotes the movement of the mind both in recognizing its own shape and in maintaining that shape in the face of attack or change. Joyce's consciousness declared itself in certain initial choices. The first came when, encountering pomp and pretence, he elected nakedness. At a point in early adolescence, he saw surrounding him an array of spiritual and secular satraps, whom he called 'Intensities' and 'Bullockships'. Rather than accept the patterns of behaviour they endorsed, he sought a primal accuracy of response, the 'utter nakedness' of which Richard speaks in *Exiles*. To keep a kind of stripped-down innocence when worldly wisdom, sanctioned by a time-worn creed and crown, was the fashion, required faith in himself and his intention. This was the faith of which he wrote at the age of twenty to Lady Gregory, 'I have found no man yet with a faith like mine' (*Letters*, I. 53).* Joyce was not the only young man in the late Victorian period to quarrel with established powers: socialists and atheists were common enough. But for him these were adjectives rather than nouns, the term they modified being 'artist'. 'It is a mistake for you to imagine that my political opinions are those of a universal lover: but they are those of a socialistic artist,' he wrote his brother in 1905 (II. 89). He had a considerable sympathy for large ideas, so long as they could be subsumed under art.

Joyce's rebellion against the Church was the first outward act of his inner resolution. As a boy he had been outraged when

---

* Quotations from Joyce's letters are unless otherwise indicated from the three-volume edition, *Letters of James Joyce*, ed. Stuart Gilbert and Richard Ellmann (New York and London, 1957–66), referred to hereafter by volume and page number only. For sources of all direct quotations not given in the text, see Notes, p. 134.

the Catholic clergy, weakkneed in politics and stiffnecked in religion and morality, aided English Gladstone in toppling Irish Parnell. He had then from the start a political concern. He was motivated also by a conviction – no less intense though it took him longer to express it – that there could be no substitute for 'the individual passion', a large term that included sexuality, 'as the motive power of everything – art and literature included' (II. 81). The point at which religious and secular morality impinged directly upon him was its demand that he restrain his sexual impulses, or, as he interpreted the doctrine, that he masturbate rather than copulate. The whole conception of sin became repugnant to him. He allowed instead for 'error'. To quarrel with the Church, as at first, according to the original draft of 'A Portrait of the Artist', he did outwardly, led him to quarrel with his mother and by extension with his motherland, in which he saw a secret collusion of Catholic and British authorities threatening hell or jail.

In late adolescence Joyce did his best to bring others into the deceptionless world he aspired to inhabit. He saw clearly that many of the notions entertained by his fellow-students, whether universal peace, feminism, or vegetarianism, were manifestations of unrest that were half-measures or off the point, and therefore delusive. The real problems were not touched, and his judgement was vindicated when even his peacetouting, feminist, vegetarian classmates (as well as bellicose, anti-feminist, and carnivorous ones) shamelessly denounced Yeats's *The Countess Cathleen* for portraying the Irish as 'a loathsome brood of apostates'. For Joyce their fulmination, which he refused to sign, exemplified subservience: they could not abide being liberated. More positively, he continually upheld to them the example of Ibsen, greatest of undeceivers and no prey to short-term enthusiasms. Joyce was filial enough to make an effort to bring his mother to his way of thinking, to persuade her, for example, that Ibsen, far from being heartless, was sacrificial; she saw the point, but distrusted foreigners. His efforts continued. Perhaps his first proselyte, aside from his brother Stanislaus, was Nora Barnacle, though, as he was ruefully aware, she submitted to his views because they were his and not because she was persuaded they were right. Eventually Joyce would make the same effort with his readers, seeking to write in such a way as to shock, confound, and amuse them into sharing his perspective.

The message Joyce had to deliver was not one that could be stated flatly. In any case, exhortation was not his way, and could not secure his goals. 'Lofty impersonal power', as he called it in his letter to Ibsen (I. 52), was more likely to succeed, even if it was sometimes mistaken for indifference. To proceed slantingly entailed reticence. Remembering how Balzac had taken for his own device and given his hero in *Le Médecin de campagne* the Carthusian motto *'Fuge . . . Late . . . Tace'*, Joyce (who had a copy of Balzac's book) prescribed for his own autobiographical hero, and for himself as well, 'silence, exile, and cunning'. For Balzac's country doctor the climactic instruction was silence, for Joyce it was cunning. Though the goal was nakedness, truth without pretences, the attainment of that goal required more subtleties than any previous novelist had supposed.

Joyce's sense of the elaborateness of his means led him to minimize his esemplastic power. If to us his imagination seems one of the most powerful in the range of literature, he did not himself think it so. He could regret, in speaking to Eugene Jolas or Jacques Mercanton, that he had relied upon fancy, moving fixities and definites about; as Mercanton remarks, the choice of the engineer Daedalus rather than of the singer Orpheus was in keeping with this point of view. In some moods Joyce accepted Vico's idea that the phantasmal faculty was essentially a function of memory: 'Imagination is nothing but the working over of what is remembered.' In *Finnegans Wake* (185) Shaun, never one to accept romantic theories of the artist, declares that his artist brother Shem writes with ink, made out of his own excretions, upon paper made out of his own skin.

But whatever impatience Joyce experienced with his own laborious methods, his ultimate theory implies more than the working over of what is remembered. Stephen comes close when he declares, in *Ulysses*, that art projects the known past and present into the unknown future: 'In the intense instant of imagination, when the mind, Shelley says, is a fading coal, that which I was is that which I am and that which in possibility I may come to be' (194; 249).* More than extrapolation occurs: there is also a process, 'erigenating from next to nothing' (as he said of Finnegan's buildings) to produce by fusion something which can never be quite what has been known and seen before.

Balzac's doctor had spoken of flight, though he fled only from the city to the country; Joyce interpreted flight more grandly as exile. To go to the Continent was to escape the illusory sins and virtues of Ireland and, for an Irishman at least, to go beyond good and evil. In October 1904 he departed with Nora Barnacle. Within six months he notified his brother that he felt entitled to consider himself 'a voluntary exile'. Being so would not only guarantee him 'a sufficiently personal future' but would also supply him 'with the note on which I propose to bring my novel to a close' (II. 84). So exile would foster his freedom to write, and at the same time provide him with a theme and a climax for *A Portrait of the Artist as a Young Man*. He would later detect in Shakespeare a note of banishment pervading the plays from beginning to end. Shakespeare's banishment was largely involuntary, or if willed, willed unconsciously; Joyce's – like that of Ibsen and Dante – was a mainly deliberate choice.

That the art he was to pursue should be literary was a decision which came easily to him. The only competing possibility was music. Joyce liked to sing poems to music, his own or Dowland's, Mangan's or Yeats's. But as he told Louis Gillet, 'I don't like music, I like singing.' In his Trieste notebook he remarks that Stephen was disqualified for a career as

* Bracketed page references following extended quotations from *Ulysses* are to the two standard editions, the one published by Random House, New York (1961) and the other by The Bodley Head, London (1960), cited in that order. References in the text to Joyce's other books are to the standard editions.

a musical performer by 'vigour of the mind', and in a notebook he compiled for the *Lestrygonians* episode in *Ulysses*, he called music 'mathematics for ladies'. The evasion of the Sirens by Ulysses was for him, as probably for Homer, a symbolical preference. Only through language could he express fully the secret life of the mind, and the secret life of the body. Music and the other arts might provide anodyne or stimulus or perception, but could not accomplish the revaluation of the world.

Language, on the other hand, working with the full resources of that world, might join things read and thought and heard of with things actually encountered. Joyce exhibits this inter-meshing in *A Portrait* when Stephen Dedalus, walking through Dublin, is reminded by the rainladen trees 'of the girls and women in the plays of Gerhart Hauptmann; and the memory of their pale sorrows and the fragrance falling from the wet branches mingled in a mood of quiet joy' (176). The sloblands of Fairview make him think of 'the cloistral silverveined prose of Newman', and Baird's stonecutting works cause the spirit of Ibsen to 'blow through him like a keen wind', and a grimy marinedealer's shop rouses in his mind Ben Jonson's song which begins, 'I was not wearier where I lay.' Joyce suggests how such memories are recomposed by the fancy when Stephen's villan-elle echoes Jonson's weariness and rhyming word with its opening question, 'Are you not weary of ardent ways . . .' Not only do 'works of art beget works of art', as Yeats said, but the landscape also plays its role. St. Stephen's Green is personalized by Stephen to become 'my green' as Slieve Bloom becomes Bloom's mountain, or – history conflating with geography – Anna Livia is the Liffey past and present. Details accumulate and, in the process of shouldering each other aside or fusing with one another, gradually change their nature. Or as Ezra Pound – another writer who thought well of fancy – imaged the process, when iron filings are subjected to the force of a strong magnet, a rose pattern forms in the steel dust.

As Joyce proceeded with each book, its scheme grew more complex in the course of embracing more and more of the world. In *Ulysses* he aspired to be both encyclopaedic and lexical; that is, the abundance of things and the abundance of words together constituted the sum total of an age. How his materials took shape, what he discarded and what accepted, what modified and what left unchanged, are aspects to be considered here. One aid to such an enterprise is his library, and some of his principal components are lodged in it. Joyce was an inveterate buyer of books. In his early years he may have spent almost as much on them as on food. The collection he put together from about 1900 to 1920 is relatively intact, in part because it left his hands. When he quitted Trieste in 1920, he turned it over to his brother; his brother preserved it, and his brother's widow did so after him. Joyce's later library in Paris survived, but because of the fortunes of war, much less integrally. Thomas E. Connolly has catalogued this later library, which is at the State University of New York at Buffalo; but some of the principal books appear to have been lost.

The Trieste library contains over six hundred items – books and pamphlets. Unfortunately, none are annotated. Some bear Joyce's signature, and quite a few bear the stamp 'J.J.', which he first used in Zurich, and left behind him in 1920 in Trieste. Although dates of purchase are rarely indicated, his letters sometimes provide information about them. Another indication comes from booksellers' marks. Joyce lived under three monetary systems, from 1904 to 1915 under the Austrian crown,* from 1915 to 1919 under the Swiss franc, and from 1919 to 1920 under the Italian lira. Where the bookseller specifies the currency, it is usually possible to establish the time span within which the book could have been acquired. Many books bear no prices; quite a few are in English, and it seems probable that these were sent to Joyce by Nora Barnacle's uncle, Michael Healy, after their first meeting in 1909.

Joyce liked to own books, and, English books not being plentiful on the Continent, he probably felt the need of a work-

* Some books marked in lire may have been purchased during Joyce's brief sojourn in Rome in 1905–6, although his impecuniosity was then at its height.

ing library in that language. He borrowed books as well, and read in libraries, but the list of his own books is large and copious enough to suggest that it incorporates most of his reading during the years 1904 to 1920. It discloses a resolution to read fairly systematically through fiction and drama. In fiction the principal names are Jane Austen, Balzac, Bandello, Björnson, Brontë, Butler, Cervantes, Chateaubriand, Conrad, Constant, Defoe, Dickens, Disraeli, Dostoevsky, Dujardin, George Eliot, Fielding, Flaubert, Fogazzaro, Anatole France, Gide, Gissing, Godwin, Goethe, Gogol, Goldsmith, Gorky, Hamsun, Hardy, Harte, Hauptmann, Huysmans, Jacobsen, Henry James, Keller, Kipling, Kock, Lawrence, Lermontov, Le Sage, Wyndham Lewis, Longfellow, Loti, Heinrich Mann, Marryat, Maupassant, Mérimée, Mirbeau, Paolieri, Poe, Praga, Rabelais, Jules Renard, Sacher-Masoch, Scott, Smollett, Sterne, Svevo, Swift, Tolstoy, Turgenev, Wells, Virginia Woolf, and Zola. Among dramatists he had works by, among others, Andreyev, Aristophanes, Barrie, Beaumont and Fletcher, D'Annunzio, Galsworthy, Goldoni, Hauptmann, Ibsen, Machiavelli, Maeterlinck, Massinger, Molière, Shakespeare, Shaw, Strindberg, Wedekind. There is poetry too, but in less profusion, by such writers as Blake, Browning, Dante, FitzGerald, Leopardi, Macpherson, Milton, Pound. Because Joyce did not leave Ireland behind him in any way except physically, there are books in abundance by his fellow-countrymen, such as Yeats, Synge, George Moore, Lady Gregory, and lesser figures such as Boyle, Colum, Macnamara, and O'Kelly. He had a spotty but not unimpressive group of books of philosophy, including Aristotle, Marcus Aurelius, Bergson, Berkeley, Bruno, Hume, Nietzsche, Russell, Schopenhauer, Thomas Aquinas. He had musical scores by Beethoven, Gluck, Mozart, Wagner. He owned Homer and Virgil in the original as well as with interlinear translations, and he had other translations of these authors as well.

Most of the subjects that come up in *Ulysses* are documented here. Writing about masturbation, he had a book entitled *Onanisme seul et à deux*. Magrini's *Manuale di musica* was helpful for the *Sirens* episode. His interest in micturition led him to obtain a book on uric acid. Was it to assist Bloom in his career as canvasser for advertisements that he secured a volume published in Chicago, *The Art of Selling Goods?* To write the *Ithaca* barrage of questions and answers, he had (as several critics have surmised) Richmal Mangnall's *Historical and Miscellaneous Questions*, which asks and answers such questions as, 'What monarchies were first formed after the Deluge?' or 'Name the great events in the first century.' For the parodies of English styles in the *Oxen of the Sun* episode Joyce assembled an impressive cluster of anthologies of English prose.

Some material for his other works is also to be found. A pamphlet, *The Prophecies of St. Malachy Concerning the Successors of St. Peter to the General Judgement, and the Destiny of Ireland*, lists the mottoes of the Popes, and a small book of poems by Leo XIII includes one in Latin celebrating the art of photography; Joyce obviously drew upon these for the story, 'Grace', which he wrote in Trieste.

Occasionally the movement from provenance to utilization is almost immediate. Joyce, bearing in mind the two chapters in which he would describe the strand, *Proteus* and *Nausicaa*, bought a book about it. This happened to be *The Common Objects of the Sea-Shore* by Revd. J. C. Wood, published in London in 1912. (An earlier edition was known to Gerard Manley Hopkins.) That he could put it promptly to advantage is indicated by the first page, where Wood describes an experiment:

Why the word 'gull' should be employed to express stupidity I cannot at all comprehend, for the gulls are very knowing birds indeed, and difficult to be deceived. If a piece of bread or biscuit be thrown from a boat, it remains but a very short time on the surface of the water before it is carried off by a gull, although previously not a bird was visible. But if a number of gulls are flying about, and a piece of paper or white wood be thrown into the water, there is not a gull who will even stoop towards it, although to the human eye the bread and the paper appear identical.

Joyce has Bloom try the same thing:

Looking down he saw flapping strongly, wheeling between the gaunt grey walls, gulls. . . . They wheeled lower, looking for grub. Wait.

He threw down among them a crumpled paper ball . . . Not a bit. The ball bobbed unheeded on the wake of swells, floated under by the bridge piers. Not such damn fools.   (152; 191–2)

So bookishness paid off.

The example is small, and the larger structures which Joyce chose to adapt were not susceptible of such immediate transplanting, especially since they could get in each other's way. Insofar as *Ulysses* depends upon literary ancestry, it is closest to the *Odyssey* and to *Hamlet*. The two chapters which follow attempt to demonstrate how Joyce assimilated these two works into his own without giving up his individuality, how in fact they gave him added power. He drew of course upon many other works, and I have named a few. To try to follow them all would be to lose the main outlines of his conscious working of materials. I have suggested how he approached his principal predecessors; various aspects of his work may appear in a new light. The last chapter seeks to present Joyce's politics under the aspect of his aesthetics, and his aesthetics under the aspect of his politics. Joyce was no closet novelist: he spoke to the world, confident that one day it would hear him. How he distorted or consolidated his materials, in the service of bringing them into a new verbal existence, is the process of consciousness which I try to investigate here.

I

Homer

1 *What's in a Name*

As a young man Joyce notified Henrik Ibsen by letter, and W. B. Yeats by word of mouth, that higher and holier enlightenment lay beyond their reach and would have to await their successors. His admiration for these writers, while great, was not unbounded: in a poem about *Ghosts* later he would twit Ibsen for his obsession with spreading guilt, and at the end of *A Portrait of the Artist* he reproved Yeats for a nostalgic aestheticism. Imposing as they were, they were already receding into the past, precursors and not saviours. Joyce saw himself as advancing beyond them into the future of literature.

Yet he stepped backward as well as forward. Why he should have adopted ancient Greek originals for both Stephen Dedalus and Bloom is more than a literary question. Like other writers, he wished to invoke the collective past as well as his personal moment. 'Ancient salt is best packing,' as Yeats remarked long afterwards. In part it was for Joyce a way of aggrandizing his characters and his country, of connecting by continental drift the Ireland which in a notebook he rudely assailed as 'an afterthought of Europe', with Greece. This anastomosis of antiquity, especially Greek antiquity, with a later age in another country, has been common enough from Virgil's *Aeneid* to Meredith's *Harry Richmond*, though rarely pursued by such intricate means.

Joyce could find encouragement in his epical aims from W. B. Yeats. In the latter's essay, 'The Autumn of the Body', included in *Ideas of Good and Evil* (1905), which Joyce had with him in Trieste, Yeats disagreed with Mallarmé that the present age would make its one medium the lyric, and argued instead for a new *Odyssey*. 'I think that we will learn again', Yeats wrote, 'how to describe at great length an old man wandering among enchanted islands, his return home at last, his slowly gathering vengeance, a flitting shape of a goddess, and a flight of arrows, and yet to make all these so different things . . . become . . . the signature* or symbol of a mood of the divine imagination.' Yeats was envisaging something on the order of his own *The Wanderings of Oisin*, in which Oisin too wanders among enchanted islands and eventually returns to Ireland. Into this fable he had woven much of his own history. But while Yeats supposed that a modern *Odyssey* would depict armed combats, Joyce had for some time been toying with a different idea, that such adventures might be internalized. He was prodded to this by a conviction that his own nature was cast in the heroic mould, although physically he was as cowardly as morally he was intrepid. Flights of arrows were not likely to issue from his bow. Yet another heroism, too everydayish to be recognized as such, might be secretly at work in a seemingly unheroic age.

The choice of an epic subject was literary without being only literary. To become a writer, one must first ask, who am I? and then, who am I not? By the age of twenty-two Joyce had put aside two careers, that of doctor and that of musician. He could now answer that he was by nature an artist, a decision he conveyed to his mother from Paris in a formal letter. It was commemorated by his conferring upon himself a new name.

Now and later, names were much on his mind. For a stage name, when he briefly contemplated that career as well, he had hit upon Gordon Brown, an English cousin of Giordano Bruno, whom he celebrated as the father of modern philosophy. But for his career as character in his own fictions, and also as a pseudonym for himself as author, he chose another name, equally magnificent in its inappropriateness. It first appeared in print as his signature to three short stories in the Irish dairy

* Yeats brilliantly converted Jacob Boehme's word 'signature', which in Boehme's *De Signatura Rerum* means God's unmistakable imprint on all things, to artistic terminology. Joyce followed him by having Stephen declare at the beginning of the *Proteus* episode, 'Signatures of all things I am here to read . . .'

cooperative newspaper, the *Irish Homestead*. To begin his career
among the curds and whey embarrassed him, and he signed
himself not Joyce but Stephen Daedalus.

While the choice may have been improvisatory, it cannot
have been any more casual than that of Gordon Brown. He
soon began to sign the same name to some of his letters demand-
ing loans, as if debts were favours bestowed by an ancient
labyrinth- and wing-maker who chose to masquerade as a
destitute young Irishman. In a letter written to his brother
from Pola, he remarked that one of his fellow-teachers at the
Berlitz School there, an Englishman, had fallen under his
'Daedalean spell' (II. 73). It was an enduring power then,
available to him abroad as well as at home. The next eighteen
years of his life were an attempt to validate this signature.

In the first of the three versions of *A Portrait of the Artist as a
Young Man* – a narrative essay written just before his twenty-
second birthday and entitled tersely, 'A Portrait of the Artist'
– Joyce avoided giving any name to his hero. Instead he called
him 'the subject of this portrait', 'the sensitive', or simply 'he',
and no doubt he wished the figure to be a little mysterious, like
'The Nameless One', the epithet by which his beloved poet
Mangan designated himself. Shying away from saying 'I',
Joyce had not yet determined upon a fictional alias, and
perhaps wished to express a disdain for mere names in the
depiction of a character who had archetypal significance. Perhaps he had also in mind the way that both Homer and Virgil
begin their epics by speaking of 'the man', no other identification being required for Ulysses or Aeneas. (Antiquity bestowed a similar distinction upon Homer by referring to him
simply as 'the poet'.)

At any rate, not naming was as deliberate as naming. In
Giacomo Joyce no name is given to the girl pupil, as if Giacomo's
indiscretion were thereby magnified and also as if her right to
be nameless derived from her compounding all desirable pupils
in one. While in the finished *Portrait* as in *Ulysses* the author
customarily calls Stephen Dedalus by his first name, such a
liberty is taken by Mr. Bloom only once in the book, and that

is when Stephen is unconscious. Bloom, for his part, is first-named only by Molly. The adventures of the name Bloom itself constitute almost a separate voyage as it steers among Bloom the dentist, Bloomusalem, Bloombella, and other variants, not to mention its translated forms Henry Flower and Virag. Homer also puns on the name of Odysseus, most famously when his hero informs the Cyclops that his name is *Outis* (nobody), but also in the verb *odyssasthai*, 'to be angry with'. 'Why do you odysseus him so, Zeus?' Athena asks her father (in George Dimock's helpful version). Joyce knew also another putative etymology, from Roscher's huge *Lexicon*, where the name of Odysseus was said by Silenus of Chios to derive from 'big ears descended from Zeus'. The big ears he did not use, nor Ovid's remark, *'non formosus erat'* (*Ars Amatoria* II. 123), but he worked out his own etymology, *outis* + Zeus, the divine nobody, at once unique and nondescript. Not the least of Joyce's affinities with Homer is the virtual obsession with naming and not naming: a chief source of interest, and a repeated one, in the *Odyssey*, is the suspense of first withholding and then disclosing the hero's name, whether to the Cyclops, to Nausicaa, to the suitors, even to his wife. A name, for both Joyce and Homer, is a weapon, a brand, an alarm.

His last book was even more name-conscious. In *Finnegans Wake* Joyce made the names of its hero and heroine pervade the book in endless variations of words beginning with their initials HCE and ALP, as Dante stamped the universe and his poem with threes to manifest the Trinity. But Joyce had a further idea in the symbol he habitually used for Earwicker, the letter E. Among the books he stamped in Trieste with 'J.J.' was one that he carried with him to Paris, Plutarch's *Morals: Theosophical Essays*, tr. C. W. King (London: George Bell, 1882). Evidently he already foresaw that one of the six essays it contained, 'On the ε at Delphi', would be useful to him. An ε was mysteriously graven on the stone of the oracle at Delphi: no one knew why. Plutarch offered a series of explanations of it, the most interesting being that the letter was pronounced like ει, Greek for 'thou art', and was addressed to the god

Apollo. The god's reply would presumably be, like that of
Jehovah in the Book of Exodus, 'I AM.' On the first page of
Finnegans Wake, Joyce unites the two phrases, when he explains
that the time was before 'avoice from afire bellowsed mishe
mishe to tauftauf thuartpeatrick', that is, before a voice from
the burning bush bellowed, 'I am, I am', in Irish, to St.
Patrick's 'Thou art'.* Joyce's letter E is a kind of all-inclusive
symbol for the human form divine, *outis*-Zeus or mangod. He
improves upon Plutarch's exegesis.

    Joyce's tenseness about naming manifested itself also in his
refusal, during the seventeen years that *Finnegans Wake* was in
the making, to disclose its title. He finally divulged it to the
frantic Faber and Faber only when the title-page had gone to
press. Goethe showed a similar reticence in refusing to let anyone read the final scene of *Faust*, which he had set aside for
publication after his death. In personal life Joyce suffered no
one except immediate members of his family and one fellow-
student (George Clancy) to call him by his first name, although
since his death some critics have been bold enough to call him
James, and I observe that an intrepid Frenchwoman, Hélène
Cixous, refers to him as Jim. (This is like calling Flaubert
'Gus'.) So long as the matter was under his control, Joyce
mistered and missused everyone and expected to be mistered
himself – a penchant for which Wyndham Lewis severely
reprimanded him in *Time and Western Man*. Lewis said it proved
Joyce was irretrievably middle-class, but perhaps it showed
only that he preferred not to rub elbows.

2   *From Daedalus to Dedalus*

To be sensitive about names was one thing, to rechristen him-

* Latent in this passage are also references to Jesus' saying, 'Thou
art Peter', to St. Patrick as baptiser (*taufen*), to tauftauf as the sound
made by bellows in a turf (i.e. peat) fire. But the Delphic reference
alone helps to explain the cryptic E.

self and his fictional self with the honorific of Stephen Daedalus was another. When he transformed his autobiographical narrative essay into its next stage, *Stephen Hero*, the new title was, according to his brother, modelled on the ballad of 'Turpin Hero'. It had its own self-consciousness, as if to rouse and then to override the idea that there were no heroes any more. I suspect, however, that Joyce had also in mind *Wilhelm Meister*, where Goethe's hero is embarrassed by his surname (Master) until he has earned the right to it. When *Stephen Hero* was in turn reconstructed as *A Portrait of the Artist as a Young Man*, the title implied that no mirror-image was meant, and that it was only one of the possible portraits that could be painted. Joyce now dropped the *a* from the diphthong in Daedalus, to diminish a little its ostentatious hellenism, and to make it more compatible with local patronymics. It remained an extremely odd name for an Irishman.

In *Stephen Hero*, so far as the surviving pages show, Joyce did not exploit the implications of the name Daedalus. That he was aware of them, however, is indicated by the fact that he pondered rewriting the book and using this time the name Daly instead. The considerable awkwardness entailed by Dedalus evidently began to worry him. He had to consider whether it might not be better to keep to the fastidious realism of *Dubliners*, a book about Dalys rather than Dedaluses. But his sense of his art as a triumph over difficulties encouraged him to prevail over this one. By the time he committed himself fully to Dedalus, at the end of 1907 or early 1908, he was much more familiar with the innovative novelists of his time, Conrad and James among them, and was eager to match their ambitious manoeuvres. He could outdo them in realism, he thought, by entering areas they shunned, and, by choosing this name from continental myth, he could dissociate himself, in the name of Europe, from symbolists like Yeats who were reviving parochial Irish myths.

The first three chapters of *A Portrait of the Artist as a Young Man* keep the magical energies of the name Dedalus in check. Stephen ponders briefly on the fact that his name is Stephen

just as God's name is God, and a classmate is allowed to take
the reader's part by commenting, 'You have a queer name,
Dedalus, and I have a queer name, too, Athy. My name is the
name of a town. Your name is like Latin.' In the last two
chapters of his book Joyce unleashes the name and thereby
tears open a new expressive region. His classmates feel its
strangeness, and mock it as Stephanos Dedalos, Bous Stephanoumenos, Bous Stephaneforos. Increasingly Stephen denies his
actual family in Dublin so as to assume kinship with his
eponymous family in Greece. To mature is to become archetypal, to recognize one's place in the roll of entrepreneurs of
the spirit. Oddly enough, the more Stephen is individualized,
the more he slips into his myth. Yeats depicts the process in
his long essay, '*Per Amica Silentia Lunae*', telling how the hero
comes to Dodona, chooses (from those lying about) a mask for
himself, touches it up here and there, fits it on, and derives
from it a strength which unmasked he did not possess.

Stephen has in fact to choose between two masks – one
Roman, that of the Reverend Stephen Dedalus, S. J., and the
other Greek. He chooses the Greek, and in these final chapters
the process of mythopoeia is accomplished like a late puberty.
More and more Stephen wears his mythical aspect. It gives
him a new perspective from which to consider his own life and
the lives around him. In comparison, *Ulysses*, where the characters are unaware of their Greek counterparts, seems guarded,
as if Joyce had concluded that, having given the later book its
extraordinary name, he might now advisedly play down the
connection. Even in *A Portrait* he devised expedients to mitigate
improbability. Temple remarks that Stephen's family is
mentioned in Giraldus Cambrensis and quotes the supposed
reference, *pernobilis et pervetusta familia*. To his friend Davin's
reproach, 'What with your name and your ideas . . . are you
Irish at all?', Stephen primly offers to take him to the office of
arms and show him the tree of the Dedalus family. The offer
has its irony, since the book is the establishment of a genealogy
for Stephen of which the office of arms knows nothing.

To accept the name of Dedalus is to accept the mission that

goes with it. 'Now as never before, his strange name seemed to him a prophecy,' we are told, and Stephen identifies himself with the winged man as a 'symbol of the artist forging anew in his workshop out of the sluggish matter of the earth a new soaring impalpable imperishable being'. This description out-does the legendary Daedalus in transsubstantiating earth as well as skimming it. For the loftier reaches of Stephen's artistic enterprise, the artificer takes on a little of Christ's power. Elsewhere in the book Stephen passingly relates the artist to God the father, so that he is not only reader of signatures – the more modest role he claims in *Ulysses* – but their inscriber, authoring a second creation with the materials of the first. The assertive role befitted Stephen's new sense of his own powers.

Ulysses was praised by Eliot for manipulating a continuous parallel between contemporaneity and antiquity. This parallel was in fact discontinuous, and included not only antiquity but other ages as well. It was not, as Eliot said in a letter, 'two plane', but three planes and more. Other writers had done it before Joyce. Eliot was to do it after him in *The Waste Land* by making images of the Fisher King, Ferdinand in *The Tempest*, the Phoenician sailor, and a contemporary Londoner coalesce with that of the prophet Tiresias, not without some echoes of *Ulysses*. Tom Stoppard, to take a more recent example, shapes the persons and incidents of his play *Travesties* by blending Joyce, Lenin, and Tristan Tzara, not to mention Joyce's antagonist in some Zurich litigation, Henry Carr, with characters in Wilde's *The Importance of Being Earnest*, and by adding touches from *Ulysses*, Gilbert and Sullivan, and the music hall. Joyce, while maintaining Greek Dedalus as Stephen's principal archetype, elsewhere in *A Portrait* relates him to Egyptian Thoth, god of writers. He was already finding it too limiting to proceed singlemythedly. The one thing needful was to loosen the grip of the plain or literal narrative without ever renouncing it, and the chosen method was to allow the hero entrance into a world of reverberations in which his own acts might be reverberant too.

Yet there was danger of undoing too much the grip of the

plain narrative. At moments when the mythical identification is strongest, Joyce humorously limits it. At the end of *A Portrait*, Stephen, about to assume the mantle of his destiny, himself laughs about the 'new secondhand clothes' which must serve as the armour for his knightly quest. Martyrdom has to be earned, by artist and by saint. Joyce forestalled (though they seem not to know it) those critics who have interpreted Stephen's departure on his mission as a blend of paranoia and megalomania, by allowing us to read Stephen's diary and see that his sense of humour – last achievement of spiritual evolution – is fully developed, and that he too recognizes how grandeur can be mere grandiosity. But Stephen ends in grandeur none the less when he prays to his adopted ancestor as to his inner self, 'Old father, old artificer, stand me now and ever in good stead.' Having put aside his biological father and fatherland, he is free to choose a mythical father in the land of his spirit. Yet he remains an Irish Dedalus as well as a Greek one.

The myth of Daedalus had, however, its limitations. His personality was vague, his participation in events narrow. If Ovid is mostly kind to him, Bacon is not. As a scientist, he was capable like other scientists of abusing his gifts. Jealous of a nephew who showed signs of matching his skill, Daedalus killed the nephew. While his invention of wings and of a labyrinth was splendid, his fabrication of a mock cow to facilitate Pasiphae's intercourse with a bull was a more ambiguous project. Joyce evidently felt that this contraption lacked dignity, and he made no mention of it in *A Portrait*, although it may be implicit in Stephen's 'monstrous reveries'. He found an explicit place for it in the ampler domain of *Ulysses*.* Another possible hitch was that Stephen, as son of Dedalus, might be taken for Icarus, who flies so badly and has no future. But Joyce suspended all reference to Icarus until *Ulysses*, where Stephen seems to pass easily between father and son, chiding himself as a lapwing (the bird into which Daedalus's dead

* See below, p. 43.

nephew was transformed) but prophetically dreaming of successful flight: 'Last night I flew. Easily flew.' In the later book the possibilities of mythical union seem almost endless, all sons and fathers being eligible, and in *Finnegans Wake* delicate discriminations among myths are no longer enforced, the melting process having gone still further.

3 *Ogygia*

Ulysses was then an extrapolation of what Joyce had learned in *A Portrait of the Artist as a Young Man*. He was able to gratify in it his love for complex structure, for a Notre Dame of literature, by parallels, arabesques, and contrasts in which his characters swell out beyond themselves only to thin once more, and then repeat the process. While he always conceived of the work, even when it was a short story, as bearing the title 'Ulysses', within a few months he discussed with his brother the possibility of making his Ulysses also an Irish Peer Gynt or an Irish Faust. In the end both these works affected it, *Peer Gynt* less than *Faust*. The relationship to *Peer Gynt* is subterranean: grim old Ibsen was in this play boisterous, and his hero more so. Peer's invasion of the untoward and unknown – among trolls, madmen, and his own depths – struck a response in a writer who regarded his art as making 'extravagant excursions into forbidden territory'.* Also to the point was the symbolical yet gnomic character of Peer's adventures, culminating in a return, perhaps more memoried than real, to a moment of youthful love which may have helped evoke Molly Bloom's recall of her courtship on Howth. Joyce was accustomed in his youth to speak of contemporary Dubliners as trolls, and the troll motto, 'Troll, to thyself be enough', suited the nationalist ('Ourselves Alone') mania of the Cyclopean Citizen in Barney Kiernan's pub. The dangers of selfhood are present also to Stephen in

* See below, p. 52.

both *A Portrait* and *Ulysses*; he avoids, however, becoming a narcissist or regarding his fellows as what Joyce in an early essay called 'the rabblement'.

The relevance of *Faust* is more pressing. Just when Joyce read it is uncertain, but possibly by the age of twenty, for in December 1902 he quotes Gretchen's song, '*Es war ein König in Thule*', from Part One. That Cohen's brothel and Goethe's Brocken have much in common was acknowledged by Joyce to Gilbert; the surrealist atmosphere, the shape changes, the mixture of pagan Helen in the classical *Walpurgisnacht* and blasphemously Christian elements (the *Dies Irae*), even details such as the *ignis fatuus*, also link the two, though the disenchantment with which each concludes has a different function.

Apart from parallel nocturnal settings, Joyce leaned upon Goethe's depiction of Mephistopheles for his own Mulligan. Mephistopheles is the spirit of denial within the universe but also, as Stuart Atkins points out, within Faust's mind. Mulligan's particular power over Stephen comes from his sharing the same thoughts, as if they were for him only shared stage props. So it is he who first sings the song from Yeats's *The Countess Cathleen*, 'And no more turn aside and brood / Upon love's bitter mystery', when it is for him neither a mystery, nor bitter, nor love. It is Mulligan who urges Stephen to join with him in hellenizing Ireland, when in fact he would only infernalize it. In the lying-in hospital Mulligan offers himself at stud to any woman in Ireland free of charge, and so, pretending to chime in with the natural fertility which the book espouses, he desecrates the love which gives fertility its point. Mulligan claims like Stephen to oppose Catholic authoritarianism and British paternalism, and he does mock them, yet at the same time he berates Stephen for not having knelt at the bedside of his dying mother, and for having failed to butter up the Englishman Haines. If he presents himself as Irish, 'all too Irish', he is quick to treat with contempt his compatriot, the old milkwoman, and is clearly destined to become, as Stephen says, one of Ireland's 'gay betrayers'.

Near the end of *A Portrait* Stephen formulates his role as 'a priest of eternal imagination, transmuting the daily bread of experience into the radiant body of everlasting life'. *Ulysses* begins with Mulligan aping this role, but transsubstantiating badly: 'A little trouble with those white corpuscles.' After Stephen theorizes elaborately in the Library about how the artist, combining in himself male and female, external and internal, brutish and spiritual, duplicates the reproductive process of nature and brings forth from his brain a work of art, Mulligan clasps his head and pretends that like Zeus he is bearing Athena from that womb. Stephen's theory of *Hamlet*, which relates the play to Shakespeare's own life, is parodied by Mulligan with his theory of art as masturbatory, 'Everyman His Own Wife'. Mulligan quarrels with the paternity theme of *Ulysses* and would recast it, when he purveys the view that Bloom's interest in Stephen is homosexually motivated, and when he mocks Stephen's promise to write a book in ten years – a commitment which Joyce (by proxy for his hero) would honour in 1914.

In action, Mulligan also behaves in Mephistophelean fashion, bullying the tower key away from Stephen and giving him the slip at Westland Row station. Essentially Mulligan, like Mephistopheles, supports the *Ewig-Leere* as against the *Ewig-Weibliche*; he says no to all spiritual effort, but at his most insidious, like Goethe's character, he pretends to say yes. In *Faust* Mephistopheles finds one of his incarnations as Zoilo-Thersites, Zoilus being the Alexandrine critic who berated Homer and took the Cyclops' part against Ulysses, and Thersites being the most foul-spoken of the Greek host. Joyce makes a similar underground connection between Mulligan and the blackhearted narrator of the *Cyclops* episode, whom, though unnamed, Joyce identified privately as Thersites. He was also Zoilus, offering a Cyclopean view of events quite different from the Irish Homer's.

Because he was conscious of following Goethe's example in devising his adversary figure, Joyce allowed himself to bow clandestinely to Goethe when Bloom, for his correspondence with Martha Clifford, calls himself Henry Flower, thus echoing

'Heinrich', the name Faust takes for his affair with Margaret.
It is Stephen, however, whose injunction to himself, 'Do. But
do', corroborates Faust's apophthegm, 'In the beginning was
the Deed.' The connections with Goethe are less overt than the
connections with Homer. They are, however, deeply ingrained.

While *Ulysses* was simmering in his mind from 1907 to 1909,
as he contemplated possible analogues with Homer, Ibsen,
Goethe, and other writers, Joyce was still in need of some
climactic event in his own life to provide motive power. He
held for himself, as later for Shakespeare, that the personal life
of the artist was all-important for his art. On 21 February 1908,
Stanislaus Joyce recorded a conversation in which Paul
Bourget's powers of psychological analysis were scouted by his
brother: 'Psychologist! What can a man know but what passes
inside his own head?' In 1909 it became apparent that the
passion Joyce needed would come from putative cuckoldry. In
that year a sometime friend, memorialized in *Ulysses* as Lynch
and identified there with Judas, impugned the fidelity of Nora
Barnacle to Joyce during their courtship five years before.
After some days Joyce's suspicions were dispelled, but the
theme of sexual betrayal was roused for good. I suspect it was
just now that Joyce saw clearly how, after having concluded
A Portrait with his departure from Dublin (1902), he could
write *Exiles* about his return to Dublin in 1909, and develop
Ulysses from his previous return (in 1903–4) during which he
had met and won his wife.

Sometime between his two trips to Dublin in 1909, as a
recriminatory letter to Nora Joyce (II. 256) discloses, Joyce
came home late one night from a café and tried to waken her
to tell her the writing plans he had framed for the future. She
was too sleepy for literary discussion. Her somnolence must
have particularly displeased him because all three works
derived a good deal of their energy from his jealousy of her.
Why should she sleep, having rendered him sleepless? As time
passed, he came to anatomize, and painfully to relish, the
sentiments which had been so unbearable. A letter from Nora
Joyce in Zurich to her husband in Locarno begins with the

salutation, 'Dear Cuckold', which indicates that it had become a marital game to tease him about the subject and so to heighten sensation. She complained to Frank Budgen that her husband was trying to force her into an affair so as to get material for the cuckoldry theme in his book. *Ulysses* was a tribute to his love, since it was set on the day in 1904 when he and Nora Barnacle first walked out together and touched each other's bodies; but it was also a tribute to his suspiciousness. He had winced too often to be sentimental.

The epic possibilities of his subject had been with him from the start. In Trieste he read in Vico that Homer, and Dante after him, were figures of *ricorso*, that stage in a historical cycle when the whole cycle could be known and leaped beyond. Vico, in his 'Discovery of the True Homer', argued that Homer was not so much an individual as the entire Greek people, with the *Iliad* and *Odyssey* representing two stages of national development. Joyce aspired to give his own work a stature and significance for the modern period comparable to Homer's in the classical period, as to Dante's in the medieval one. *A Portrait of the Artist* belonged to the old stage and *Ulysses* to the new one.

In his reading Joyce began to find unexpected confirmation of his procedure. Remarkable coincidences seemed to confirm that the Homeric analogy could provide a key to the world. At the beginning of the *Odyssey* Ulysses is on Calypso's island, Ogygia. This was the name that Plutarch gave to Ireland, and was the title of a well-known early history of the country by Roderic O'Flaherty, *Ogygia, seu, rerum Hiberniarum Chronologia* (1685). Such intermeshing made clear to Joyce that he had a right to his epic parallel. He set about multiplying these correspondences.

I know that some readers, including Ezra Pound, have discounted parallels with the *Odyssey* as mere scaffolding. Joyce ventured to disagree. It is of course true that he is not on his knees before Homer. As Samuel Butler said of Homer, in an essay Joyce had read,

He was after all only a literary man, and those who occupy themselves with letters must approach him as a very honoured member of their own fraternity, but still as one who must have felt, thought, and acted much as themselves. He struck oil, while we for the most part succeed in boring only; still we are his literary brethren, and if we would read his lines intelligently we must also read between them.

But if Joyce did not abase himself, he deferred. When he began to serialize *Ulysses* in the *Little Review*, he insisted that Homeric titles be prefixed to the episodes. Later he expunged these, but they remained in his mind if not on the paper. Before and after publication day he circulated to his favourite critics one or other of the two schemes he had prepared, in which the Homeric titles continued to identify the episodes. In writing to his aunt Josephine Murray, whom he was anxious that the book should please, he urged her (I. 174) to read first a prose version of the *Odyssey* before tackling his own book. When she was slow to comply, he repeated (I. 193) after publication the same instruction he had given earlier. Stuart Gilbert's book, and Frank Budgen's, both written under Joyce's eye a decade after *Ulysses* had appeared, kept also to the Homeric pattern. In later life Joyce sometimes reversed this process, and responding to Vladimir Nabokov's respectful comments about his knowledge of Homer, he disclaimed any special acquaintance with the *Odyssey* or with Greek. To those who read the book as an ordinary work of fiction, he wished to make clear its elaborate structure; to those who addressed themselves to the structure, he pointed to the novelistic element. This is no more than to say that DNA is based upon the double helix and could not exist without it.

The broad outlines of Joyce's narrative are of course strongly Homeric: the three parts, with Telemachus's adventures at first separate from those of Ulysses, their eventual meeting, their homeward journey and return. Equally Homeric is the account of a heroic traveller picking his way among archetypal perils. That the *Odyssey* was an allegory of the wanderings of the soul had occurred to Joyce as to many before him, and he had already designated the second part of a book of his poems as 'the journeyings of the soul' (II. 20). He had also construed

Stephen's progress in *A Portrait* as a voyage from Scyllan promiscuity in Chapter II to Charybdean simonpurity in Chapter III, and to reconciliation in Chapter IV. Although in *Ulysses* he diverged sharply from Homer in the order of events, Joyce clearly adapted the Homeric settings and what he chose to consider the prevailing themes. He found the *Odyssey* beautifully all-embracing in its vision of human concerns. His own task must be to work out the implications of each incident like a Homer who had long outlived his time and had learned from all subsequent ages. Joyce once asked his friend Jacques Mercanton if God had not created the world in much the same way as writers compose their works; but he then bethought himself and murmured, 'Perhaps, in fact, he does give less thought to it than we do.' Neither God nor Homer could compete with Joyce in self-consciousness.

Although Joyce was modest about his knowledge of ancient Greek, he had more than a smattering of it and did not neglect the classical infusion of his material which could be secured through language. On the principle I have mentioned, of letting the adversary propel, however crookedly, the book's themes, he has Mulligan quote tags from Herodotus and Homer, and after mentioning *epi oinopa ponton*, the winedark sea, has him invent two post-Homeric epithets, the snotgreen and scrotumtightening sea. The very first words of the book, 'Stately plump Buck Mulligan' instead of the more normal English order, 'Buck Mulligan, stately and plump', seem to homerize English, as do more consciously Greek epithets such as 'bullockbefriending bard'. The description of the Citizen in the *Cyclops* episode as 'a broadshouldered deepchested strong-limbed frankeyed redhaired freelyfreckled shaggybearded wide-mouthed largenosed longheaded deepvoiced barekneed brawnyhanded hairylegged ruddyfaced sinewyarmed hero', salutes the epithet even while mocking it. The *Aeolus* episode offers two sentences which sound like an exercise in Homer's formulaic composition: 'Grossbooted draymen rolled barrels dullthudding out of Prince's stores and bumped them up on the brewery float', followed by 'On the brewery float bumped

dullthudding barrels rolled by grossbooted draymen out of
Prince's stores.' Joyce seems determined to burst the confines of
English by allying it with the stylized language in which Homer
clothes his mythical materials, or by a linguistic innovation as
radical as Dante's decision, in another *ricorso*, to use the vernacular. *Finnegans Wake* best realized the latter aspiration. He
began now his habit of taking out the space between compound
adjectives, a small hellenization to which he subjected *A
Portrait* in its last stages as well, and also a new edition of
Chamber Music. While Homer's use of traditional phrases and
archaic forms could not be precisely duplicated, Joyce achieved
something of the same effect by having his characters quote
well-known phrases from past authors.

In cementing his bond with Homer, Joyce soon realized that
he must become familiar with Homeric scholarship. Commentators could draw his eye to particulars which he might otherwise
overlook. The three to whom he attended most closely were
Butler, Bacon, and Bérard – an unlikely trio, but no less handy
for that reason. Critics who have mentioned the importance to
Joyce of one or other of these commentators have not taken
into account how opposed to each other they were. Joyce had
to decide which of them to follow, and faced with this decision,
he tended as was his wont to follow them all, up to a point.

He said later, in a letter (I. 401), that he had encountered
Bérard only when he was three-quarters through his book; his
library in Trieste also suggests that Joyce used Butler and
Bacon first. Of Butler he read both *The Authoress of the Odyssey*
and *The Humour of Homer*, as well as *Erewhon* and *Erewhon Re-
visited*, in which there are Homeric overtones. Butler had a
radical conception of the poem and its geography and author-
ship. For him Homer was not an Athenian but a Sicilian, that
is, a Greek living in a settlement in Sicily, and moreover, not a
man but a woman. The voyages which Butler sketched for
Ulysses all took place in or near Trapani. That Homer was a
woman and no sailor was proved for Butler by amateurish
details; so Ms. Homer describes Ulysses' placing a rudder on
his raft 'to steer by', as if a rudder might have some other

function. Bérard, however, thought Ulysses an expert seaman.

Victor Bérard, later the dean of French classicists, could in fact hardly have been more at odds with Butler. His huge work in two volumes, *Les Phéniciens et l'Odyssée*, which he published in Paris in 1902 and 1903, took issue as well with all established theories. For Bérard Homer was by no means the Greek people (he specifically opposed Vico on this point); instead he was a cosmopolitan man, a Greek working with foreign materials. As a landlubber, like other Greeks, Homer knew nothing of the western Mediterranean, where most of the action of his poem occurred; he therefore relied upon the sailing manuals of the Mediterranean's best sailors, who were the Phoenicians, a Semitic people. In Bérard's view, Homer was a Hellene, Ulysses a Phoenician rover. Joyce could conveniently assume that all Semites were alike, Phoenicians and Hebrews being for his purposes (if not for history's) interchangeable, and so he could claim Bérard's authority for that climactic encounter in *Ulysses* when 'jewgreek meets greekjew'.

Bérard attributed to Homer the same painstaking accuracy of description that Joyce sought to attain, and in fact made him a Joyce of the classical age. Bérard's Homer invented nothing, though he sometimes combined a mainland scene with one on an island. (Bérard does not allow Homer to be fanciful, that is, inaccurate, by more than a sea mile or two.) Like Joyce, he worked with fixities and definites. Bérard's main contribution, and what he considered the key of his work, was the doublet, which he claimed was the basis of Homer's epic. For the Greek names given by Homer to various places made no sense in Greek, but in Hebrew and Phoenician made perfect sense. As an example, Circe's island is called by Homer Nesos Kirkes and also Aiaia. Aiaia means nothing in Greek, but in Hebrew means the island of the She-Hawk. From this Homer devised the toponym, Nesos Kirkes, which means she-hawk in Greek. To allow for a more complex provenance, Bérard suggested that Homer may have worked with an Egyptian epic based upon a Phoenician sailing manual. In other words, the whole Middle East played its part.

If Joyce had had to evaluate these scholars as scholars, he might well have been sceptical of both. Butler's theory flew in the face of traditional associations of places throughout the Mediterranean with scenes in the *Odyssey*. Bérard's theory worked with such associations as far as possible, but to make them tally with Homer urged modifications of Homer's text – interpolations or omissions or transpositions – and claimed that many important passages, such as Menelaus's battle with Proteus, were spurious. But Joyce liked the idea of a Semitic original for the Greek poem, and he welcomed Bérard's insistence that Homer was a realist and not a fabulist. The poem offers a stable world of scenes described at secondhand, often inaccurately, but on the best authority.

What Butler saw in it was, however, helpful too. He gave the poem a homely familiarity by locating its scenes, just as confidently as Bérard, on Sicily and small islands nearby. No sailing manual was needed: the places were all instantly recognizable still. This view required even more special pleading than Bérard's, as when Butler insists that the whole voyage from Phaeacia to Ithaca was only a mile or two. While Joyce did not have to believe that the *Odyssey* was written by a woman, he had already come to the conclusion that every artist is a womanly man or manly woman. Butler's identification of the woman author with Nausicaa encouraged Joyce to allow both Nausicaa and Penelope to have their say in his own book, and he tested out Butler's contention that the principal female figures were aspects of one person rather than separate beings. Finally, Butler insisted, as Bérard denied, that the *Odyssey* was just like other fictional works in being covertly autobiographical: the events in it arose out of the circumstances of the authoress's life, the people in it were people she knew, and some of them could be identified even at a distance of almost three millennia in time. Joyce concurred, in so far as the origins of his own book were concerned.

A third item in Joyce's Odyssean kit was Francis Bacon's *The Wisdom of the Ancients*, which Vico also found useful. Joyce had two copies of it. Bacon differed with both Bérard and

Butler by disdaining to see any naturalism or autobiography in the *Odyssey*. For him the book was a method of imparting intellectual lessons through fables. That is, Bérard and Butler treated the fabulous as factual; Bacon, with Vico after him, treated the factual as fabulous. Instead of hunting for the location of Scylla and Charybdis, Bacon held that Homer meant to illustrate by this emblem the rocks of distinctions and the whirlpool of universals. Joyce accepts this Baconian symbolism, modifying its details as needed. I think he was also impressed by the legend, which Bacon retails with scepticism, that Penelope was unfaithful to Ulysses not with one suitor alone but with all of them, the offspring of this large-scale mating being Pan or universal nature. This legend, and others like it, encouraged Joyce to make his Penelope, Molly Bloom, unfaithful too, to compile a list of her lovers as long as Don Giovanni's but more putative than real, and to allow her in her reverie to run through an epic history of fallen man, like Michael's to Adam in *Paradise Lost*.

Following Bérard, then, Joyce patiently established geographical details and made his poem like Homer's a melting pot of the races. Following Butler, he saw in the poem an extrapolation of Homer's autobiography, for which he could more or less substitute his own. Following Bacon, he found both voyage and voyager to be symbolic. Thanks to these scholiasts and others, the reading of the *Odyssey* offered admission to a drama of violent disagreement.

4   *Ulysses' Last Voyage*

Another form of commentary on the *Odyssey*, besides scholarly exegesis, was its sequels. The final voyage of Ulysses, which Tiresias had prophesied and Homer had chosen not to provide, became a subject for later writers. Joyce accepted Dante's view that Ulysses sailed beyond Gibraltar on a last voyage, but instead of shipwrecking him on the Mount of Purgatory he brought him safely to Ireland's shores. Aside from Dante, four post-Homeric treatments of this theme won his attention.

The first, a ludicrous one, but fully accepted in the epic cycle of Greece, was the *Telegony* written by Eugammon of Cyrene about two centuries after Homer. Eugammon dispatched Ulysses on a shorter voyage than Dante's, to the land of Thesprotia, where the hero marries the queen Callidike. That Joyce had Eugammon in mind is proven by the scheme of his own book which he sent to Carlo Linati in September 1920. He indicates there that Molly Bloom serves in the fourth chapter as both Callidike and Calypso, as if to combine Eugammonic and Homeric treatments. From Joyce's point of view, on Butler's principle of the implicit union of Homer's female characters, Molly Bloom might be seen under these aspects as well as under those of Penelope or Nausicaa. The later history that Eugammon presents, if Proclus's summary of the lost epic can be trusted, had a kind of perfunctory unity. Callidike bears Ulysses a son and dies. When the son is grown, Ulysses, having heard that some young man is ravaging Ithaca, returns to his own country. He does not know that the marauder is really Telegonus, his son by Circe, who is in search of his father. Failing to recognize each other, the two do battle and Ulysses is killed. Telegonus, having discovered his mistake, takes his father's body and, accompanied by Penelope and Telemachus, brings it to Circe's island for burial. Circe confers immortality on Telemachus and Telegonus; then Telemachus marries her while Telegonus marries Penelope. Eugammon was ready to tie up loose ends at any cost. Joyce had a study of the lost *Telegony* in his library; what interested him particularly was the reiteration in the sequel of the theme of a son searching for his father: Telegonus is as pessimistic a version of filial piety as Telemachus is optimistic. Joyce was mindful also of the incestuous joining of Penelope and Telegonus, and probably found there a hint for Molly's quasi-incestuous fantasy about Bloom's quasi-son Stephen. The presence in the *Telegony* of three sons of Ulysses encouraged Joyce to give Bloom two.

To some extent Joyce wished his book to be a sequel to the

Odyssey, to some extent a re-enactment of it. The best model for both was Virgil's *Aeneid*, which followed the *Telegony* by seven hundred years. Joyce had copies in his library of this work both in the original and in translation. Though Virgil wrote from the point of view of Ulysses' adversaries, the Trojans, he followed Homer none the less, as typologically as the New Testament follows the Old. Virgil, like Joyce after him, changes the order of the episodes, but retains many of them in somewhat altered form. Calypso becomes Dido, and Aeneas descends to the shades not to see his mother, as Ulysses did, but like Bloom in Nighttown to see his father. Other incidents could also be displaced. If Aeneas meets in Hades an angry Dido, Bloom might meet in Circe's palace, which is hellish too, all the women about whom he feels guilty. But the principal Virgilian connection was the incident of the Trojan horse, which Homer did not present. Joyce's handling of this, as will appear, was exceedingly multiform.

In more recent times, Joyce found support in an unexpected quarter, Fénelon's *Les Aventures de Télémaque*. This attempt to present the model rearing of a model young man does not sound like Joyce's sort of thing, and W. B. Stanford, in his fine book on *The Ulysses Theme* (1963), gives it scant notice. But Joyce had Fénelon's book in his library, and found in it an imitation by Telemachus of Ulysses' adventures which could not fail to be useful. Télémaque too goes to Calypso and he too must escape her toils. He too is shipwrecked. For Joyce this parallelism could suggest the nub of his own treatment, that Ulysses and Telemachus, instead of voyaging independently, might put in to the same ports. (Meredith's Harry Richmond also blends Ulysses and Telemachus.) Fénelon's book was in eighteen episodes, another point in which Joyce eventually followed him. In the eighteenth the young man and his father at last meet, an encounter heralded throughout the book. But Fénelon handles it in a remarkably muffled way: his Telemachus does not learn until after Ulysses has departed that it was to his father he was speaking. It is one of those resonant unfulfilments, like Wordsworth's discovery that he has crossed the Alps without knowing it. Joyce had here an unusual precedent for the equally resonant and yet extremely muted ingathering of Bloom and Stephen.

On the basis of all or most of this reading, Joyce embarked on his own work. In using the *Odyssey* as his model, he knew he was risking everything. Nothing easier than to founder on that rock. To name it *Ulysses* was like calling one's book the Bible.

There were certain restraints upon him. He had to keep his new work separate both from *A Portrait*, which he finished in 1914, and from *Exiles*, which he began in 1913 a few months before he commenced the actual writing of *Ulysses*. Since one of these works dealt with a dramatic departure, the other with an equally dramatic return to Dublin, his new hero might best be kept inside the city from beginning to end. Not only must Homer's sea become dry land, but physical exploits must be made less sensational. The only bloodletting at the end of Joyce's book is menstrual. Joyce might have simply intellectualized Homer, as Bacon did, but he did not intend to give up the physicality of the *Odyssey* altogether. Certain incidents which did not show Ulysses at his most winning or magnanimous, however, Joyce was glad to omit. For example, the first stop of Ulysses, in the land of the Ciconians, ends in the slaughter of the men and the sharing of the women, diversions interrupted by the arrival of Ciconian reinforcements. This savage treatment was perhaps inserted by Homer to offer a foretaste of Ulysses' vengeance, and to surround the tale of his adventures with a ferocity which most of the intervening incidents do not permit him to exert but only to suffer. Joyce left out the Ciconians altogether.

Some adventures could be abridged: one visit to Circe was enough (Homer has two). But other incidents were expanded, the Lotus-Eaters for example, where in an atmosphere of *dolce far niente* Bloom like the rest whiles away his time, at moments bathing in inconclusive sensation as Ulysses does not, yet converging with Ulysses in his close scrutiny of the individuals he meets and the institutions to which they belong. When he decided to make the climax of his book the visit to Circe's brothel, rather than the return to Penelope's Ithaca, Joyce did not surrender this contrast altogether: his Nausicaa, though her own innocence is somewhat qualified, is islanded between two foul-mouthed episodes.

I imagine Joyce as reading and re-reading Homer with a special delight because of his own ulterior motivation. He testified to his pleasure in the episode where Ulysses, grizzled and scarred, or as Joyce said to a friend, 'perhaps baldheaded', yet still eligible, is a suppliant before the virginal seventeen-year-old Nausicaa. That the shipwrecked man should be naked made Joyce think of emphasizing what he called 'the parts that mattered' by Gerty's coyness about them. Homer's hero, after having covered these parts with a leafy branch, addresses the princess in fulsome style, 'I kneel to thee, Queen, are you goddess or mortal?' This is blarney but it works. Nausicaa responds to these attentions by indicating how very mortal she is, so mortal indeed that she is quite prepared to marry him if asked. Joyce adapts Homer so that Gerty's mortal-immortal being is evoked by a similar confusion between the original Gerty seated on the strand and the Virgin Mary ensconced in the Star of the Sea church nearby. Coy miss and sacred myth interact. Votive offerings are made to the two shrines simultaneously. These elements were present in Homer, though admittedly latent. Joyce not only brings them to the surface, but couches them in a style which, at once adulatory and lubricious, seems also to be asking with Ulysses, 'Are you goddess or mortal?'

The rationale of making Ulysses Irish was more difficult. That the Irish were like the Greeks no one will deny; what western people is not? The earliest invaders of Ireland, the Firbolgs, were legended to have come from Greece. A scribal note in the *Book of Armagh* (folio 22, column a) makes a claim which Saint Patrick himself abstained from making in his *Confessio*, that he was the great-grandson of Ulysses. Joyce sports with this putative ancestry in his book. What was more extraordinary was to make Ulysses not simply an Irishman but

an Irish Jew. I will not trace here Joyce's developing interest
in the Jews, but besides having Jewish friends in Dublin, he
became in Trieste the English teacher of a large number of
Jewish pupils. Among them was Ettore Schmitz (Italo Svevo),
a fellow-writer of genius, from a family which like Bloom's had
migrated from Hungary; like Bloom, too, Svevo had married a
Gentile who was part Jewish. Svevo was as witty as Oliver
Gogarty, but without malice; much of his humour was turned
upon himself, and his books explored amorous contretemps in a
way that Joyce admired and learned from. The personality
of Svevo gave Joyce the impulsion he needed to form a new
character, a blend of Svevo, himself, and other prototypes.

More largely, the Wandering Jew was in Joyce's mind, as it
was in his library in Eugene Sue's version. (He had also read
Heijermans' *Ahasver* and Mark Twain's less reverent treatment
of the same subject in *The New Pilgrim's Progress*. Other wan-
derers such as Wagner's *The Flying Dutchman* played their part.)
So was the idea of the oldest people wandering in exile century
after century and still maintaining, in spite of oppression, an
identity. Although Joyce did not read Bérard's conception of a
Semitic *Odyssey* until he was well advanced on his book, in
Dublin before he left in 1904 he had come upon another writer
who could offer him support. This was the eighteenth-century
comparative mythologist, General Charles Vallancey, a
follower of Jacob Bryant. In a lecture he gave in Trieste in
1907 (included in *Critical Writings*), Joyce cited Vallancey's
theory that the Irish were of Phoenician origin. It appeared
that Vallancey and Bérard, each unknown to the other, had
made both Greeks and Irish Semitic. It was as difficult not to
be Jewish as not to be Greek.

But no Dubliner of Joyce's generation had to rely upon
scholars for the comparison of the Irish to the Jews. In October
1901, at a meeting of the Law Students' Debating Society,
John F. Taylor made the famous speech in which he brilliantly
compared the Hebrews in Egypt to the Irish under foreign
domination. Joyce probably heard the speech: it was said at
University College that his own oratorical manner was like

Taylor's. But in any case he had access to *The Language of the Outlaw*, a four-page leaflet published privately but in large numbers (5,000 or 10,000 copies) in 1904 or 1905. The pamphlet explained that the only record of Taylor's remarks was contained in a letter to the *Manchester Guardian* signed 'X', which it then reprinted:

Sir,—May I venture to send you a few words as to a speech made by Mr. J. F. Taylor last November at the University College Debating Society? . . . The discussion was on the question whether the Irish people might be allowed to know or take an active interest in their own language. Lord Justice Fitzgibbon had made a dialectical discourse of a kind with which we are all familiar on platforms. . . . After his conventional fireworks Mr. Taylor rose. He had been very ill, and had come straight from his bed, and without food.

He began with some difficulty, but his power increased as he went on. . . . He compared, in one passage, the position of the Irish language under English rule to the position of the Hebrew language under Egyptian rule. He set out the arguments which a fashionable professor with an attachment to the Egyptian Court might have addressed to Moses:—

'Your prejudices are very antiquated and sentimental', he would have said. 'Do just look at the matter in a reasonable light, like a man of the world. Here your people have been now for hundreds of years in the brickfields. The fact is patent that they have never been able to rise out of this miserable position.

'They have no education; the mass of them are poor, demoralised, and despised. They have no history outside their brickfields, and within them they are the foolish prey of agitators who set them clamouring for straw. Instead of adopting the enlightened and philosophic religion of Egypt, they still cling through all these generations to a superstitious and obscurantist faith, mischievous and altogether behind the times.

'Their language is rude and provincial. It is incapable of expressing philosophic thought.

'It is, of course, useless for commercial purposes. As for literature, the fragments that remain are well known to be either superstitious or indecent – in any case quite unfit for ordinary people.

'You must recognise that the interest your race attaches to it is derived from mere ignorance and obstinacy; it would be quite unworthy of a man of culture, and certainly impossible in a man of the world or moving in society. Consider, on the other hand, the Empire to which you now, happily for you, belong – its centuries of civilisation, its ancient history, its buildings, its arts, its literature. Observe its splendid Imperial organisation, its world-wide fame, its ever-increasing dominions, its satisfactory foreign relations with the Great Powers, the lustre of its achievements, which put it for ever in the rank of one of the greatest Empires which the world can know to the end of time. Why, then, do you not frankly throw in your lot with this magnificent and successful organisation? A handful of obscure peasants as you are, you would at once share in its renown and its prosperity.

'Of course you could depend on being generously treated by rulers of such standing. Something would doubtless be done for those poor labourers of the brickfields. More favourable terms could be made for them – who knows? A supply of straw at a reasonable price; security of tenure of their mud huts; lower rents even.

'The deserving could enter the Egyptian service, or make a start in commerce, or learn industry from this great and progressive country. Only get rid of those brickfield agitators. Give up your outlandish and useless language. Reconsider your superstitious sort of religion. Put an end to all this nonsense, quite out of place in good society – to local dialects, out-of-date provincial patriotisms, and illiterate sentimentalities which Providence itself condemns by casting them out into mud huts and brickfields and acre holdings.

'And,' broke out the speaker, 'if Moses had listened to those arguments, what would have been the end? Would he ever have come down from the Mount with the light of God shining on his face and carrying in his hands the Tables of the Law written in the language of the outlaw?'

Joyce welcomed the analogy even if he spurned the argument for Irish against English. The language movement did not appeal to him at all, and in fact was the point where he felt at odds with the separatist movement. But it was a great speech, and Joyce designed a great answer to it. He put the description of Taylor's speech in the mouth of Professor MacHugh, and ventured to improve upon its style, while at the same time casting doubt upon its content. MacHugh follows the *Guardian* letter in first introducing Mr. Justice Fitzgibbon's speech:

—It was the speech, mark you, the professor said, of a finished orator, full of courteous haughtiness and pouring in chastened diction, I will not say the vials of his wrath but pouring the proud man's contumely upon the new movement. It was then a new movement. We were weak, therefore worthless.

Then begins some of the elaborately observed stage business which gradually asserts itself as a countermovement to oratory:

He closed his long thin lips an instant but, eager to be on, raised an outspanned hand to his spectacles and, with trembling thumb and ringfinger touching lightly the black rims, steadied them to a new focus.

IMPROMPTU

In ferial tone he addressed J. J. O'Molloy:

—Taylor had come there, you must know, from a sick bed. That he had prepared his speech I do not believe for there was not even one shorthandwriter in the hall. His dark lean face had a growth of shaggy beard round it. He wore a loose neckcloth and altogether he looked (though he was not) a dying man. . . .

—When Fitzgibbon's speech had ended John F. Taylor rose to reply. Briefly, as well as I can bring them to mind, his words were these.

He raised his head firmly. His eyes bethought themselves once more. Witless shellfish swam in the gross lenses to and fro, seeking outlet.

He began:

—*Mr chairman, ladies and gentlemen: Great was my admiration in listening to the remarks addressed to the youth of Ireland a moment since by my learned friend. It seemed to me that I had been transported into a country far away from this country, into an age remote from this age, that I stood in ancient Egypt and that I was listening to the speech of some highpriest of that land addressed to the youthful Moses.*

His listeners held their cigarettes poised to hear, their smoke ascending in frail stalks that flowered with his speech. *And let our crooked smokes.* Noble words coming. Look out. Could you try your hand at it yourself?

—*And it seemed to me that I heard the voice of that Egyptian highpriest raised in a tone of like haughtiness and like pride. I heard his words and their meaning was revealed to me.*

FROM THE FATHERS

It was revealed to me that those things are good which yet are corrupted which neither if they were supremely good nor unless they were good could be corrupted. Ah, curse you! That's saint Augustine.

—*Why will you jews not accept our culture, our religion or our language? You are a tribe of nomad herdsmen; we are a mighty people. You have no cities nor no wealth: our cities are hives of humanity and our galleys, trireme and quadrireme, laden with all manner merchandise furrow the waters of the known globe. You have but emerged from primitive conditions: we have a literature, a priesthood, an agelong history and a polity.*

Nile.

Child, man, effigy.

By the Nilebank the babemaries kneel, cradle of bulrushes: a man supple in combat: stonehorned, stonebearded, heart of stone.

You pray to a local and obscure idol: our temples, majestic and mysterious, are the abodes of Isis and Osiris, of Horus and Ammon Ra. Yours serfdom, awe and humbleness: ours thunder and the seas. Israel is weak and few are her children: Egypt is an host and terrible are her arms. Vagrants and day-labourers are you called: the world trembles at our name.

A dumb belch of hunger cleft his speech. He lifted his voice above it boldly.

—But, ladies and gentlemen, had the youthful Moses listened to and accepted that view of life, had he bowed his head and bowed his will and bowed his spirit before that arrogant admonition he would never have brought the chosen people out of their house of bondage nor followed the pillar of the cloud by day. He would never have spoken with the Eternal amid lightnings on Sinai's mountaintop nor ever have come down with the light of inspiration shining in his countenance and bearing in his arms the tables of the law, graven in the language of the outlaw.

He ceased and looked at them, enjoying silence.

(141–3; 179–81)

Against this euphony Joyce and Stephen assert a reality principle. MacHugh belches. His glasses are full of witless shellfish seeking outlet. Stephen thinks, 'Noble words coming', and when they have come, tersely comments, 'Dead noise.' His one voiced reaction is to invite the company for a drink. On the way to it he tells his own 'Parable of the Plums' as foil to Taylor's parallel, as the blade of truth amid the airbags of oratory. There is no Moses on Pisgah, there is no promised land, only two old women spitting out plumstones on Dublin from the top of Nelson's pillar.

Joyce did not accept Taylor's argument for the Irish language, but he welcomed with all its shortcomings the analogy of the races. It would seem that Hebraism and Hellenism, far from being opposites as Arnold and Auerbach have contended, had been brought into touch by the theories of Bérard, and Celticism with them by the theories of Vallancey and Taylor. The imagery of Moses and the Promised Land was in fact a cliché of revolutionary poems and songs of the period, as Louis Hyman informs me. Joyce's compatriot, Oscar Wilde, had urged 'a new hellenism', and in his early critical writing Joyce spoke with only the faintest irony of Ireland's becoming 'the hellas of the north'. It is part of Mulligan's obtuseness that he can at once urge Stephen to join with him in hellenizing the island, and not perceive the secret affinity of Greece and Palestine. To be anti-Semitic, as Mulligan is, is to challenge the foundations of Joyce's book.

Joyce was aware that the conjunction of Greek, Irish, and Jewish had a humorous aspect. He depicts Bloom as eager to incorporate Aristotle, whom Stephen so much admires, into the Hebraic tradition, on the grounds that Aristotle had received instruction from a rabbi, whose name has somehow slipped Bloom's mind. But if there was a humorous aspect to this and other matters, it was comedy of a special sort, comedy with teeth and claws. Vico had pointed out that Homer was not a delicate writer, delicacy being too small a virtue for so large a mind. Joyce was not eager to be delicate either. To hellenize the island meant to combat its dark insularity. As Hegel noted, a belligerent situation is the one most suited to epic. Joyce dismissed the idea of devoting half his book, as Homer had done, to vengeance, and even countered Homer by bringing Bloom to complaisance rather than to indignation over his wife's adultery. But he hit upon the plan of combining the assault upon the suitors with the adventures of Ulysses. A war, even if undeclared and bloodless, is waged from the start.

5   Ulysses Redivivus

That war was not to be waged by Ulysses alone. Faced by the example of Homer, who had begun his epic with Telemachus, then dropped him to take up the thread of Ulysses' wanderings, then brought the two together to wreak destruction, Joyce embarked on a different course. The counterpoint of Bloom and Stephen might be a source of greater interest if neither was allowed to upstage the other. Consequently Joyce altered the relations of Ulysses and Telemachus: he shared out the attributes of Ulysses between them. There are not one but two Ulysseses. (He says so explicitly in naming to Linati the characters in the *Aeolus* episode, where for the first time Bloom and Stephen appear to be working in tandem.) Together, though unwittingly so, they wage the battle of Dublin, the attempt to instil a foreign conscience into their native city. And since the return to Penelope's arms is not so conclusive in *Ulysses* as it is in the *Odyssey*, Joyce makes his Ulysses and Telemachus reach what he mysteriously called (in the scheme sent to Carlo Linati) a state of 'fusion'. That word suggests not that they disappear in each other, but that they coincide; they converge as component parts of the whole. They do not have to change in order to come together, only to detect resemblance. They companion each other unconsciously in most of the book, consciously in three of the four chapters at the end, the fourth and last being reserved for Molly Bloom to link them once and for all in her mind. They are not opposites, their relation is rather like the yolk (Bloom) and white (Stephen) of the egg, with Molly as the enclosing shell.

Just as blood relationships fade in *A Portrait*, so they fade in *Ulysses*. Simon Dedalus is never discharged from his paternal role, but he is supplemented by Bloom, who, though he is milder than Simon Dedalus in expression, sharply anatomizes the prevailing forces of Dublin and dissociates himself from them, as Simon Dedalus, for all his scathing wit, does not. Once he had accorded to Bloom a symbolic paternity, Joyce felt free to take advantage of the parity of his two leading characters, and to vary Homer accordingly. In the *Aeolus* episode, for example, Homer has Ulysses' crew pierce the bags of wind while Ulysses sleeps. The parable was one of greed. In Joyce's version, however, both Bloom and Stephen pierce the windbags of Dublin, and the parable is one of fustian. Similarly, Homer's Telemachus never reaches Circe's palace, except in Eugammon's sequel; Joyce has them meet in Circe's palace and resist her wiles together. Certain adventures are not shared, or not patently shared. It might seem that the *Lestrygonians* and the contiguous *Scylla and Charybdis* chapters separate the two men. But in fact these chapters are constructed in tandem. In the first Bloom has to taste his way between the opposing perils of vegetarianism and cannibalism, alimentary equivalents for the sentimental and the pitiless, and does so by choosing, compassionately, a Gorgonzola sandwich with a glass of burgundy. The cheese is derived from mammals without slaughter, and yet is alive; the bread, and the wine too, are reconstructed from vegetable matter by men. Bloom has also to remember his way between lubricity and etherealism when he recalls, in this same chapter, how sixteen years before he lay with Molly among the rhododendrons on Howth, and by genuine feeling avoids the perils of lust and idolatry, too much salt or too much sugar. In the second of these chapters, Stephen has to intellectualize a way between the brutality of physical fact and the ethereality of spirit; he discovers that this may best be achieved, since the two are dangerous only in isolation, by mating them. In terms of Homeric gastronomy, neither a mollycoddle Shakespeare nor a wholly brutal one can be digested, but only one who combines these extremes in a humanistic completeness. The Gorgonzola solution, for food, love, and art, is arrived at by both men.

In the second half of the book, Joyce begins by allowing both Bloom and Stephen to negotiate the Wandering Rocks, chiefly by keeping clear of both viceregal and secular authority. The three chapters that follow centre on Bloom, but they bear a covert relation to Stephen. In the *Sirens* Bloom plays out, under the aspect of Homer, the events Stephen has described in Shakespeare's life: his humiliation as cuckold, his abortive love affair. Boylan will have Molly and Bloom not have Martha. But it shows Bloom also parrying both sentimental love, in the song 'Martha, thou lost one', and sentimental hate, in 'The Croppy Boy'. Then in the *Cyclops* episode Bloom comes head on against the anti-Semitism which Stephen has opposed in the earlier chapters, and against the nightmare of history as force which Stephen has also exposed. Bloom defends himself as a Jew, and condemns physical force, while the Citizen espouses anti-Semitism and physical force and attempts to combine them against Bloom. (Stephen's parallel endangerment from physical force comes in the *Circe* episode.) As for Bloom's adventure with Gerty MacDowell in the *Nausicaa* episode, this orchestrates the simpler theme of Stephen's fancied possession of his muse on the strand in *A Portrait*, and its brief harmony of young and old anticipates the more genuine concert of young Stephen and old Bloom in subsequent chapters. The orgasm achieved simultaneously by Bloom and Gerty, without touching each other, shadows forth the feats of artistic engendering, carnal yet not carnal, at the end of *Circe*. The four episodes that follow *Nausicaa* give Bloom and Stephen the opportunity to demonstrate their accord on principal questions, and after their parting at Eccles Street they are once more joined, and for ever, in Molly Bloom's mind.

As Joyce plunged into his work he re-read Homer in the way that Virgil must have done, looking for Homeric details that might be expropriated. He found some curious ones. For example, Homer in the *Iliad* describes Ulysses as having short legs and a long upper torso; this detail lurks behind the funny walk with which Joyce endows Bloom ('Shitbreeches, are you doing the hat trick?' cries the motorman as Bloom dodges out of the way). Telemachus sneezes in the *Odyssey*, portentously as it turns out; a character in *Ulysses* has a fine sneeze as well, though less charged with significance. For many details Joyce evolved a whole series of correspondences: *moly*, for instance, the flower which Hermes gives to Ulysses to protect him from Circe's magic, signifies everything from potato and garlic on the one hand to luck and prudence on the other. The Trojan horse, so prominent a part of the Trojan war in Virgil, might be thought a detail impossible to copy. But here too Joyce found the equivalences or near-equivalences he needed.

To begin with, he dotted his books with references to horses, from the first page where Mulligan's face is 'equine in its length', and continuing with Boylan (who is Bloom's antitype as Mulligan is Stephen's) as son of a man who not only unpatriotically sold horses to the British during the Boer war, but – treachery within treachery – sold them twice over. Molly is 'a gamey mare and no mistake'. Then there is the horse race that day: Boylan bets on Sceptre, but it is the lowly Throwaway who wins, as Bloom had unwittingly prophesied earlier. (In his true witness he betters Dante's Ulysses, who burns in hell because of bearing false witness about a horse.) Joyce's larger view of the matter is expressed by Joe Hynes when he says of Bloom in the *Cyclops* episode, 'He's a bloody dark horse himself.' That is, he is an innocuous-seeming man whose independence of spirit mines the city, whether the city knows it or not. This view of him is held up to examination by ridicule in the brothel scene, when Bloom, like Aristotle in the medieval legend Joyce quotes, is 'bitted, bridled, and mounted' by Bello Cohen. He is measured and found to be fourteen hands high. The society ladies promise to dig their spurs into him up to the rowel. His womanly manliness makes him describe the tangle he is in as 'a pure mare's nest'.

Joyce does not leave Stephen out of this imagery. It is Stephen who pulls together the Trojan horse designed by Ulysses with the wooden cow designed by his precursor Daedalus, when he speaks of Helen as 'the wooden mare of Troy in whom a score of heroes slept. . . .' Not all these hoof-beats of the Trojan horse can be heard – Joyce did not mind so long as the book thudded with them. And in a way the book itself, as well as its two principals, was a Trojan horse, parading as a monument, but, as will later appear, armed for battle.

So Homer lent himself to adaptation, and the Homeric adventures and heroes become pliant under Joyce's hand. He tried to make his book thick with all the hidden possibilities of his material. Yet at a certain point Homer and his 'unchristened heart' did not suffice as Joyce's example. The clarity, the movement across seas and years, the sequentiality, the Attic light – these were all very well, and Joyce sometimes imitates them, notably in his book's first chapter. But as Coleridge said in his *Table Talk* (12 May 1830), 'There is no subjectivity whatever in the Homeric poetry.' Joyce had in mind another movement, which might be called vertical as against Homer's horizontality, and which would be characterized not so much by progression as by a furling and refurling of thought. All that could be seen and heard could be called into question by all that could be felt and fancied. Homer would be his warp; someone else had to constitute Joyce's woof. That easy, un-trammelled quality for which Homer was justly celebrated had to be detailed, retarded, and even opposed. Or, to put it another way, paganism had to be checked by post-paganism.

II

Shakespeare

1 *Unnatural Murder*

The *Odyssey* begins with a murder case. Heaven, as well as
Greece, still reverberates with the 'soldier's pay' which Agamemnon, like Ulysses a returning veteran, has received at the
hands of his wife and her lover Aegisthus. The after-effects are
even worse, and the gods in conclave on Olympus discuss the
most recent homicide, Orestes' vengeful murder of Aegisthus.
They are too polite to mention that Orestes has killed his
mother as well as her lover. Joyce's characters exist also against
a background of violence, though they are not violent men.
Even Earwicker, as he re-enacts the Fall, appears to be guilty
of peccadilloes rather than capital crimes. Two celebrated
murders, one from literature and the other from life, impinge
upon Bloom and Stephen. The one from literature is *Hamlet*. In
his inveterate multiplying of instances, Joyce could see Hamlet
as roughly parallel to Orestes, another prince avenging a royal
father's murder by an adulterer. The element in the murder
case at Elsinore which was missing from the one at Argos was
that Claudius was brother to King Hamlet. It was just this
element which Joyce, evidently feeling a need for local parallels,
chose to reinforce by frequent references to an actual case in
Dublin in 1899, when a man named Childs was accused of
having murdered his brother. Together, the Hamlet and the
Childs cases constituted the analogue Joyce sought for his book.

By crossing Homer with Shakespeare, not to mention other
elements, Joyce established a kind of parallax to his own time,
as viewed from the two points of the classical age and the
Renaissance. Virgil had sutured together the *Iliad*, *Odyssey*, and
Argonautica, but all were set in the remote past. For his

contemporary material Joyce needed some intermediary between ancient and modern. In adopting *Hamlet*, he enormously
complicated his task. The intrusion of *Hamlet* into Homer was
awkward since Telemachus and Hamlet, while both in some
sense avengers, had quite different situations. In particular,
Penelope was, at least according to Homer (for ancient gossip
told a different tale), as faithful as Gertrude presumably was
unfaithful; and if Hamlet's father was dead, Telemachus's was
very much alive. As for Stephen Dedalus, he was not in a
position to wreak vengeance upon anyone, neither upon his
mother's lover (for she had none) nor upon his uncle, with
whom he was on excellent terms. When like Orestes he is
accused of killing his mother, he only momentarily allows the
charge to lie, and later formally denies it: 'Cancer did it, not I.'
(Joyce himself accepted a measure of guilt over his own mother's
death: as he wrote Nora Barnacle on 29 August 1904, 'My
mother was slowly killed, I think, by my father's ill-treatment,
by years of trouble, and by my cynical frankness of conduct',
and Nora Barnacle, as Joyce's Trieste notebook records, called
him 'Woman-killer' (an epithet also conferred on Richard by
his wife in *Exiles*).

It is hard to imagine anyone but Joyce proceeding in the face of
so many difficulties. He remarked to Jacques Mercanton, '*Il n'y a
qu'une feuille qui sépare* Ulysses *de la folie*,' and then, more hope-
fully, '*La seule chose qui me permette d'achever, c'est la parole de Blake*:
"If the fool would persist in his folly, he would become wise." '
If in spite of difficulty he insisted upon compounding his book
with *Hamlet* as well as with the *Odyssey*, it was because he sensed
latent affinities with both, and recognized that for his purposes
neither would do alone. Telemachus in Homer was an innocent,
on the dull side, not least because he lacked Stephen's most
convincing attribute, that of being an artist. Hamlet had no
such shortcoming. Although in the play the only artistic works
attributed to him are a high-flying stanza to Ophelia, a speech
in the play within a play, and a doggerel verse after, he is still
the type of the artistic hero. As such, he has been the darling of
writers.

His adoption as a second prototype for Stephen was not less temerarious for that reason. Most writers since Shakespeare who have presented young men as heroes have been eager to minimize the influence, and have made their heroes say with Eliot's Prufrock, 'No, I am not Prince Hamlet, nor was meant to be.' Skirting the character of Hamlet has been part of the labour of writing a *Bildungsroman* or *Kunstlerroman*. Stephen disdains such a disavowal, and to emphasize his compatibility with Hamlet Joyce itemizes Hamlet's component parts. So Stephen wears a Hamlet hat, mourns for a dead parent (though the wrong one), calls for tablets on which to write, feels that Mulligan is a pretender, says, 'Hamlet, revenge!' as well as 'To have or not to have. That is the question.' His formulation of a theory of the play *Hamlet* becomes not just an intellectual excursion, but a theory which applies to *Ulysses* as well. Just as there are two Ulysses in the book, there are sometimes two Hamlets: Bloom falls into venerable Hamlet expressions such as 'There's the rub', and he, rather than Stephen, meditates possible revenge for adultery. After having viewed a billboard announcement that Mrs. Bandman Palmer will play *Hamlet* that night as a male impersonator, Bloom speculates, like the scholar Vining, on the possibility, 'Perhaps he was a woman. Why Ophelia committed suicide?' Later he impersonates a woman himself. Just as, in joining forces with the *Odyssey*, Joyce spotted his book with references to Cassandra, Helen and Paris, Ulysses S. Grant, Greek statues, Troy measure, so he spreads Shakespearean references, not only to *Hamlet* but to the other plays and to Elizabethan people in dense profusion.* Penelope Rich refers back to poor Penelope. As Bloom says of Shakespeare, 'Quotations every day of the year. To be or not to be. Wisdom while you wait.'

Joyce felt more than most writers how interconnected literature is, how to press one button is to press them all. He exhibits none of that anxiety of influence which Harold Bloom

---

* One reference, 'What's Hecuba to him or he to Hecuba', over-bubbled into a poem, 'A Memory of the Players at Midnight', where Joyce envies them: 'They mouth love's language.'

has recently attributed to modern writers. Yeats said, 'Talk to me of originality and I will turn upon you with rage.' If Joyce had any anxiety, it was over not incorporating influences enough. In *A Portrait of the Artist* (180), Stephen fears he will always be but a shy guest at the feast of the world's culture; in *Ulysses* Joyce plays host to that culture. In his library was Georges Polti's *Les Trente-six situations dramatiques*, in which hundreds of works, and some incidents of history and modern life, were conflated to show that all made do with three dozen basic plots. This was a literal working out of Joyce's contention in his undergraduate paper, 'Drama and Life', that the laws of human society are changeless. That one hero should gall the kibe of another seemed therefore second nature. Joyce knew that Ulysses' voyage was not the first of its kind, that it followed, for example, Jason's. Similarly he thought he might accept Shakespeare as companion up to a point, much as Dante had accepted Virgil, and Virgil Homer, up to a point.

Since Hamlet was mostly to be equated with Stephen, Hamlet's father must resemble Bloom. Joyce was spurred on by a theory of *Hamlet* that he had begun to frame in 1904 – he drew as widely as possible for his book upon the congestion of incidents and ideas in that year. This was that the dead king rather than the living prince wore the lineaments of Shakespeare. In the twelve lectures that he gave in Trieste in 1912–1913, he developed this theory of the relation of the play to Shakespeare's life. The lectures have been lost, but a newspaper account appears to confirm that this was their direction. What he proposed was to study the play not in itself but as an expression of its author. For in middle life Joyce celebrated not the 'lofty impersonal power' of the artist, but the intimate tie between work and life. He enforced the theory that great literature was necessarily autobiographical, his examples being the novels of D'Annunzio and the plays of Shakespeare.

He might, it's true, have put Dante in Shakespeare's place. The classical world could have been balanced by the medieval rather than the Renaissance world. Like Goethe in *Faust*, Joyce does not ignore the medieval world. He makes frequent

allusions to it, and draws upon Thomas Aquinas and others.
Most of all, his book is tinctured with Dante:* the three parts
of *Ulysses* are more than vaguely equated with the three books
of *The Divine Comedy*: the first chapters, in which Stephen feels
damned and among the damned, are followed by a long series
of purgatorial adventures culminating in the total purge of
Circe, and these in turn are followed by glimpses in the last
episodes of a lost paradise. In a way Joyce's book was itself a
Dante exploring spiritual states in this world, and classifying
human creatures in a way foreshadowed by Stephen in *Stephen
Hero*, who decides that his contemporaries would fit appropri-
ately into particular circles of Dante's hell. As Mary T. Reynolds points out, the flames surrounding Ulysses, which to
Dante appeared like those about Ezekiel in his fiery chariot,
are adapted, less seriously, for the end of the *Cyclops* episode,
when Bloom ascends unsinged to heaven. Joyce also went to
great trouble to situate Molly Bloom's childhood on Gibraltar
so that the last voyage of Ulysses, which Dante described as
through the pillars of Hercules, could be enacted in her
imagination as she remembers her first lover on the Rock of
Gibraltar and her principal Irish one (Bloom) on the Hill of
Howth. Ulysses ships by fantasy from one eminence to another
across the seas, and Molly's circumnavigating imagination
guarantees that an Odyssey has really taken place.

Other aspects of Dante were not workable here. Joyce gave
the name of Beatrice, with some wryness, to the hero's spiritual
mistress in *Exiles*, but it could scarcely be conferred upon the
more earthly love of Bloom. Nor was Dante's sense of sin
appropriate, although Joyce allows Stephen some of those
vestiges of Christian feeling which he had himself. (Thomas
McGreevy recorded in some never published notes that during
a thunderstorm in Paris Joyce, always terrorstricken on such
occasions, was trying to dive under the furniture of his flat,
when a friend remarked, to bolster his courage, 'Look at your

* See Mary T. Reynolds, 'Joyce's Planetary Music: His Debt to
Dante', *Sewanee Review*, 72 (Winter 1964), 450–77, for many connections, and her forthcoming book on the subject.

children; they're not frightened at all.' The agnostic Joyce replied with contempt, 'They have no religion.') But although he was able to say in his less uxorious moments that he had never loved anybody but God, and in Trieste even intimated to his brother that he thought everyone retained some faith in a supreme being, he anchored himself in unbelief. Dante was then less apt to his purposes than Shakespeare, whose ethics were secular, the sense of Christian sin largely replaced by guilt and remorse. (Joyce found hints also in Yeats's stories of the secret rose, which he learned by heart, where to express or fail to express one's being are the new terms for what used to be virtue and sin.) For Joyce Shakespeare was not a Christian humanist but a post-Christian one, a man like himself, schooled in doubt, caught between Stratford and London as he was caught between Ireland and the Continent, tormented by jealousy, prone to be betrayed, his pen the only weapon of reprisal he had against a world which misused him. Joyce liked also that for Shakespeare, as for himself, literature was a method of possessing and repossessing the denseness of being, of which all events conspired to dispossess him.

At the same time, Joyce's relation to Shakespeare had its strains and stresses. In *Finnegans Wake* he lumped him unceremoniously as one of the trio of Daunty, Gouty, and Shopkeeper, emphasizing that bourgeois status to which Stephen attends when he says that 'Shakespeare drew Shylock out of his own long pocket'. For Joyce this was only a mock-slur, and implicitly a recognition of kinship. In youth Joyce disparaged Shakespeare for lacking Ibsen's dramatic sense, and objected, like Voltaire before him, that Ophelia's madness duplicated Hamlet's and so weakened it. But by the time he wrote *Ulysses*, he had thought better of this criticism, and had Bloom encounter not one madman but two, Breen and Farrell, while Stephen for his part contemplates the careers of two other madmen, Swift and the Abbot Joachim.

In assimilating *Hamlet* into the fabric of his own book, Joyce had the encouragement of Goethe. The resemblances between *Faust* (Part One) and Shakespeare's play were extraordinary, and Georg Brandes had specified them in his life of Shakespeare from which Joyce quoted in 1913 in his last lecture on *Hamlet*. Brandes calls attention to the similarity of the relationship of Faust and Margaret to that of Hamlet and Ophelia. Both represent, as he says, 'the tragic love-tie, between genius and tender girlhood'. (Joyce had Ophelia and Margaret as well as Nausicaa in mind when he framed the character of Gerty MacDowell.) Faust kills Gretchen's mother as Hamlet kills Ophelia's father, a cue that must have prompted Joyce to have Stephen labour under the charge of having killed his own mother. The interchangeability of one parent with another is as basic to Joyce's plan as is the interchangeability of Ulysses and Telemachus. In both *Hamlet* and *Faust* a duel takes place between the hero and his mistress's brother, in which the brother is killed; in both the girl in her misery goes mad. As Brandes points out, the song of Ophelia that begins, 'Tomorrow is Saint Valentine's day', is paraphrased in Mephistopheles' sardonic song, '*Was machst du mir*'.

As valuable to Joyce as *Faust* was Goethe's use of *Hamlet* in his novel, *Wilhelm Meister*. Joyce quotes from the latter, if only to disagree with it, but it showed him how he might incorporate in a novel areas of the play and also commentary on it. Wilhelm Meister, beginning a career as an actor, chooses *Hamlet* for his first vehicle. Not only does he play the role on the stage, but in a larger sense he *is* Hamlet. The network of relationships extends to minor details so that Wilhelm's father like William Shakespeare's has just died, and the unknown actor who plays the Ghost resembles him. A woman who plays Ophelia actually commits suicide. A man named Laertes plays Laertes. The similarity centres above all on the leading characters. For Wilhelm Hamlet is a man like himself, having a nature too sensitive for the part fate has assigned to him; he lacks the 'sensuous strength which makes a hero', and, in a famous passage to which Joyce makes Lyster refer, Hamlet is described as an oaktree that bursts its costly containing vessel.

For Stephen Hamlet has a different artistic temperament, one more like Stephen's than Wilhelm's in its ruthless severity.

The Joycean Hamlet resembles the old king who when alive smote the sledded Polacks on the ice. The artist is violently moved by love and hate, spurred on to revenge – bloodless revenge, perhaps, but no less satisfying for that. Violence is violence, even within the covers of a book. This view, shared between Stephen and Joyce, dispels the conception of *Ulysses* as an indulgent book. It is no more indulgent than *Hamlet* or the *Odyssey*, although it worsts its adversaries without making corpses of them.

2   *Two Ghosts in* Hamlet

In 1916 Joyce entered in a notebook a dream that Nora Joyce had had, which he interpreted in his own quasi-Freudian manner:

At a performance in the theatre
A newly discovered play by Shakespeare
Shakespeare is present
There are two ghosts in the play.
Fear that Lucia may be frightened.

Interpretation: I am perhaps behind this dream. The 'new discovery' is related to my theory of the ghost in Hamlet and the public sensation is related to a possible publication of that theory or of my own play. The figure of Shakespeare present in Elizabethan dress is a suggestion of fame, his certainly (it is the tercentenary of his death) mine not so certainly. The fear for Lucia (herself in little) is fear that either subsequent honours or the future development of my mind or art or its extravagant excursions into forbidden territory may bring unrest into her life.

The strangest thing in the dream play is that it is *Hamlet* with two ghosts instead of one, yet this is the detail for which Joyce offers no gloss. If he considered explanation gratuitous, some explanation is needed for that attitude. It must be presented roundabout.

Stephen's aesthetic theory in *Scylla and Charybdis* begins with a declaration of the toughmindedness of artists. His second contention is that the composition of *Hamlet* was no spinning of semiotic signs, but an act of mirroring Shakespeare's life. Earlier in the book he had presented his Parable of the Plums, in which he signalled the sterility of Ireland as promised land. This was the external world, *tout court*, in which as artist he found himself. His second Parable, of the Horns, seeks to establish in what indignities Shakespeare's work took on its stance and colouration, or in other words, how his predecessor's internal life reflected his external life. Essentially Stephen maintains that Shakespeare thought of himself as King Hamlet's Ghost – the role he actually took in the play – and translated into Danish the English humiliations he had endured. In the symbolic mode of a historical, physical murder, Stephen declares, Shakespeare recounts the spiritual victimization he has been made to suffer. That victimization had begun when his wife Anne Hathaway committed adultery with his two brothers, and worsened when his best friend stole from him the dark lady.

The terms are symbolic because Shakespeare had been poisoned in mind rather than in body, by the discovery of disloyalty in those closest to him. He did not revenge himself with a knife, but with a play, and in the play his swordsman son became the instrument of his revenge. For the play contained a second ghost: Shakespeare resurrected for its Oresteian tragedy his dead child Hamnet, no longer a boy of eleven years as when he died, but a solid wraith, fat and thirty, wreaking vengeance in the flesh (so far as the play was concerned) which his father could wreak only in the spirit. So the play is a revenge play doubledyed, being Shakespeare's psychic revenge upon his victimizers as it is his reanimated son Hamnet's physical revenge upon them. The historical and geographical setting is a cover for a timeless spaceless event taking place in Shakespeare's brain. His vindictive passion is a reality so strong that it requires a whole cast and stage to express itself.

To work out this theory Joyce had to consider problems of psychology as well as of Renaissance life. Among the books he possessed in Trieste were three small pamphlets in German, published in the years 1909 to 1911. The bookseller's price for these is in crowns in each case, so that Joyce certainly had them in his possession before he left Trieste in 1915. But the proximity of their publication dates, as well as their ephemeral nature as pamphlets, suggests that he acquired them about the time they were published. One of them is Jung's *The Significance of the Father in the Destiny of the Individual*, just the subject that Stephen explores. (Jung modified it later to give more prominence to the mother.) The second is Freud's *A Childhood Memory of Leonardo da Vinci*, where the relation of early memories to works of art is displayed with great subtlety, and bears out Joyce's view of the intimate relations that could be detected between, say, the portrait of Mona Lisa (of which he had himself once written) and childhood experience. The third essay must have startled him: this was the earliest version of Ernest Jones's celebrated psychoanalytic theory, *The Problem of* Hamlet *and the Oedipus Complex*, then just translated into German. It has usually been supposed that Joyce encountered the influence of Freud and Jung later, when he was in Zurich during the First World War. His interest certainly continued into that period, to judge from his dream notebook and also from his purchase then of a copy of Freud's *Psychopathology of Everyday Life*. But his possession of the three pamphlets I have mentioned strongly suggests that he knew about psychoanalysis several years before, I suspect from the time that Italo Svevo's relation by marriage, Edoardo Weiss, introduced psychoanalysis into Italy, that is, by 1910.

The relevance to Joyce of this new way of thinking about the mind can hardly be overstressed. The three essays 'burst in upon his porcelain revery' with their transformations, combinations, and divisions of the self, their picture of its abasements and suppressed appetites and ambivalences, which were as yet largely untapped for conscious literature. It must have been clear to Joyce at once that he had here a new continent. He had always tried, even in his youthful conception of the literary epiphany, to detect the moments when the mind unwittingly

gives itself away in casual speech. Freud systematized this kind
of epiphany with his theory of slips of the tongue. In his story,
'The Sisters', which was pre-Freudian, Joyce used the mala-
propism of rheumatic (for pneumatic) wheels, but this cross-
contamination is merely funny, and similar examples could be
found in any Irish dialect novel of the nineteenth century.
When Bloom speaks of 'the wife's admirers' and means 'the
wife's advisers', however, we are in the age of Freud. The
psychoanalytic pamphlets helped Joyce also to envisage a more
precise genetic account of two forms of action, one the act as
externally lived, the other the act of writing about it. The
mind's seethings towards external event, and towards reconstruction of that event in words, might be traced with
precision.

Joyce reserved this analogy for the climactic episode of
Circe, where the memories and fantasies of Bloom and Stephen
attain a violence of humiliation and aggression, and then of
artistic recovery, comparable to those in the Homeric and
Shakespearean adventures. Their minds generate both inward
and outward occurrences. Outwardly Stephen breaks the lampshade in the brothel with his walking stick, inwardly he defies
his mother's ghost and seeks to banish that perturbed spirit to
the grave in the name of his independent spirit and with the
aid of Siegfried's sword, *Nothung*. Bloom outwardly rescues
Stephen from Nighttown, and inwardly imagines his dead
child alive again. Freud makes this interweaving of life and
literature much more viable than it had been before.

The Freudian theories also tended to break down the
hierarchy of virtues and vices against which Joyce had already
begun to campaign. 'Monstrous images' of sexuality and death
were distributed democratically through the world, the prim
sharing them with the depraved. Joyce always maintained
what he wrote to his brother from Rome in November 1906,
'if I put down a bucket into my soul's well, sexual department,
I draw up Griffith's and Ibsen's and Skeffington's, and Bernard
Vaughan's and St Aloysius' and Shelley's and Renan's water
along with my own.' One touch of kinkiness makes the whole

world kin. What he did other people did too, with whatever variations, but only he had the courage to say so. To be peculiar was to be human.

Even if Joyce did not subscribe to Freudian theory as doctrine, it assisted him in his aim of presenting in secular terms, disinfected of theology, spiritual struggles once thought to be private matters between a man and his priest. It suited him, too, in that Ernest Jones, following Freud, saw *Hamlet* as the product of Shakespeare's own dilemmas, and gave the prince a complex with a classical name, Oedipus, wonderfully parallel to Joyce's own efforts to give Stephen a Daedalus complex. Later Joyce would give him a Hamlet complex as well. Everyday relations of father and mother and child took on for Freud, as for Joyce, the proportions of classical drama, while at the same time remaining phantasmagorias within the individual mind.

When it came to the Oedipus complex, Joyce was not prepared to submit to Freud's theory. Freud held, and Jones expanded the idea, that Shakespeare wrote *Hamlet* in the period following his father's death when his Oedipal feelings were sharpened by grief, so that it is Shakespeare's own Oedipus complex with which the prince is burdened.* For Jones the play is basically one of youth revolting against old age: Hamlet, in love with his mother and jealous of his father, envies his uncle for having done what he himself wished to do. His envy is unconscious – hence his hesitation about revenge, and his rationalizations of delay. Jones holds that neither Shakespeare nor Hamlet knew what the real trouble was, neither suspected the impulses which Freud would lay bare some three centuries later.

Stephen's theory is almost the opposite of Jones's. He refers, a little anachronistically for 1904, to the theory emanating from Vienna and dissociates himself from it. His Shakespeare is

---

* Strangely, Ernest Jones in this first version of his essay does not mention Gertrude's adultery, although A. C. Bradley, whose work he cites, had already emphasized it. Eventually it became a mainstay of Jones's argument.

fully in command of the situation. The central character in his play is the dead father, not the living son. King Hamlet is jealous of his wife for her adultery, and to a lesser extent of his son for his youth. That by the end of the play both are as dead as he seems to follow. But Prince Hamlet, as presented by Stephen in *Ulysses*, shows no telltale sign of lust for his mother or of jealousy for his father, nor does Stephen himself. (In the same way, Stephen, faced with another father figure, the Polonius-like Mr. Deasy, headmaster of his school, fences with him but draws no blood and is basically kind to him.) Joyce disagreed, then, with Jones and Freud about the Oedipal situation, probably because he found little trace of it in himself. He preferred the filial Greeks to the parricidal (and matricidal) ones, Telemachus and Ulysses (for Ulysses also is a son in the book) to Oedipus and Orestes. So for all its classical parallels, the book *Ulysses* is held apart from Freud's classical model of family relations as Joyce had sampled it through the three essays.

As he pondered the new version he was writing of *Hamlet*, in which Shakespeare came forward from the wings and virtually took over, as ghost, the whole play – *Hamlet* without the prince – Joyce made some daring transformations. The wound of being cuckolded which he attributes to Shakespeare is shared with Bloom. Although at the end of *A Portrait* Stephen was suffering from a friend's interest in his beloved, he is represented here as without cause for sexual jealousy. Bloom was given no brothers nor any close friend to betray him, as if Joyce wished the parallel to be inexact. But to make up the lack, Stephen has treacherous friends if not a treacherous brother. Joyce provided Bloom also with a son, lost not like Hamnet Shakespeare at eleven years but – by one of many jarring, deliberately imperfect resemblances – at eleven days. Shakespeare had two daughters, and Bloom is allowed only one, to keep the situation simple, and perhaps again to make the similitude only partial. The approximateness of these resemblances helps to explain why, in the *Circe* episode, when Bloom and Stephen look into a mirror together, they see not their own faces but the beardless face of Shakespeare, 'rigid in facial paralysis'. William M. Schutte proposes that Bloom and Stephen together 'amount only to a paralytic travesty of a Shakespeare'. But for them to fuse altogether with Shakespeare would deprive them of their own places in the sun. Whenever resemblances become especially close, Joyce warns us that he is working with near-identities, not perfect ones, approximating each other at some remove, as a left glove resembles a right. Pressed too far, the analogies become comic near-misses, as here, rather than sober hits.

The combination of Homer and Shakespeare in Joyce is so unexpected that one would think the affinity would be constantly threatened. Yet on the contrary, there are many moments when it seems almost predestined, so deftly are the influences intertwined. For example, Stephen, gazing at Mulligan as the first chapter ends, thinks, 'Usurper'. The epithet is one he is entitled to use, because Mulligan is asserting proprietary rights over the tower, but it is equally one to which Telemachus, surrounded by the suitors, is entitled: and Hamlet as well, suffering from his uncle's usurpation of the kingdom. The martello tower is said by Haines to be like Elsinore, and it is also like the high place where Telemachus in the *Odyssey* has his room. Mr. Deasy is Homer's Nestor; he is also Shakespeare's Nestor in *Troilus and Cressida*, and he is Polonius in *Hamlet*. Ulysses' father, like Ophelia's brother, is named Laertes.

Everything conspires to help Joyce. Stephen makes another of these weird conflations when he says, 'Bring a stranger within thy tower it will go hard but thou wilt have the secondbest bed', at once a reference to Antinoos and the other suitors of Penelope, to King Hamlet and cuckoldry, to Shakespeare and his possibly ironic legacy of the secondbest bed to Anne Hathaway, to Stephen's resigning his own bed in the tower to Haines, and to Bloom's partial loss to Boylan of Molly's attentions. As Bella Cohen says, 'You have made your secondbest bed and others must lie in it.' Joyce's Penelope offers her husband a secondbest bed as at first does Homer's. Sometimes these connections become exceedingly tangled: for example, the ghost Mrs. Dedalus, like King Hamlet's ghost, speaks of hellfire, but she threatens Stephen with it as the king's ghost does not do; by a kind of chiasmus it is Bloom who encounters a *father*'s ghost, yet not a terrifying one. And while Stephen is the primary receptacle for the artistic side of Shakespeare, Joyce wishes Bloom also, in his character as 'old slyboots' (an epithet both Molly and Circe confer on him), to have a 'touch of the artist' about him.

3 *Some Versions of Hamlet*

In his able book on *Joyce and Shakespeare*, William M. Schutte has established that Joyce drew upon three particular books, the biographies by Sidney Lee, Georg Brandes, and Frank Harris. It must now be added, however, that Joyce had upwards of a dozen books on Shakespeare in his flat in Trieste, and several editions of the plays. For example, he had J. Dover Wilson's *Life in Shakespearean England*, which ends with a characterization by Nicholas Breton in *Fantastickes* of each hour of the day – such as Joyce was to devise for himself. One book which proved especially helpful to Joyce was an unlikely source, a small volume that made part of a series entitled *Days with the Poets*. This was *A Day with William Shakespeare*, by 'Maurice Clare', the pseudonym of a prolific writer of the period named May Byron. It was published by Hodder and Stoughton on or about 1 November 1913 (the date recorded in the Bodleian copy), and I suspect found its way to Joyce soon after. Maurice Clare deftly incorporates some information about Shakespeare's lodging with a Huguenot family in Silver Street; these details had only recently been discovered, in 1910, by Charles William Wallace. The book begins:

It was early on a bright June morning of the year 1599.

Joyce has Stephen say,

It is this hour of a day in mid June.

Clare goes on,

The household of Christopher Mountjoy, the wig-maker, at the corner of Silver Street in Cripplegate, was already astir.

Stephen moves on more quickly,

Shakespeare has left the Huguenot's house in Silver Street and walks by the swanmews along the riverbank.

Then Maurice Clare gives a hint which Joyce exploited to the full. He says,

To these good folk . . . entered their well-to-do lodger, Mr. William Shakespeare.

I have looked at many of these little books by Maurice Clare, which deal with other well-known figures in literature and art, and this is the only one to introduce the hero as *Mr.*, as if Maurice Clare too felt that Shakespeare's shopkeeper status was in need of formal attestation. This may well have been the comic inspiration for Joyce's presenting us not to Mr. Shakespeare but to Mr. Leopold Bloom, a solecism which clings to him like a Homeric epithet throughout the book.

Maurice Clare like Stephen deals with Shakespeare at thirty-five, and emphasizes that he was well past his youth:

Mr. Shakespeare was thirty-five years of age, 'a handsome, wellshap'd man', in the words of his friend Aubrey, – his eyes light hazel, his hair and beard auburn. . . . In the seventeenth century people aged soon, and thirty-five was more like forty-five nowadays.

Stephen calls him

a greying man with two marriageable daughters, with thirtyfive years of life, *nel mezzo del cammin di nostra vita*, with fifty of experience . . .   (207; 266)

thus matching up Shakespeare with Dante (as Joyce matched himself with both in his letters to Martha Fleischmann in Zurich). One thing that Stephen has Shakespeare do is to pay a visit to his friend Gerard the herbalist. The source for this is Maurice Clare, who speaks of the fine garden-ground Gerard

had in Fetter Lane* and has Shakespeare call on Gerard.
Stephen puts this more brilliantly:

In Gerard's rosery of Fetter lane he walks, greyedauburn.

(280; 362)

The garden is specified to be a rosery to make Shakespeare fall
in line with the rose and flower imagery associated with the
Blooms in the book. Stephen's sentence about Gerard is inter-
jected again in the *Sirens*, where it seems to have no relevance
except to remind us that Shakespeare, even when not on stage,
waits in the wings, and Stephen with him. It also suggests that
Joyce is orchestrating the narrative with added extravagance.

Maurice Clare brings Shakespeare on his walk to the Globe
theatre where the play of *Hamlet* is in rehearsal, but gives
Shakespeare the role of Rosenkrantz rather than that of the
Ghost; she then takes him to bookstalls near by in St. Paul's
churchyard, then into St. Paul's itself. Joyce sends both Bloom
and Stephen to bookstalls, and sends Bloom into All Hallows'
church. Later Shakespeare is represented by Maurice Clare as
brooding on his illassorted marriage, his wife left behind in
Stratford, his shortlived affair some time back with a dark
lady; to conclude the day, Shakespeare meets his brother
Edmund, dines at the Mermaid, and goes home through the
fields. The outline of Bloom's day and thoughtful peregrinations
is similar. His dark lady is Martha Clifford, his Anne Hathaway
is Molly. Maurice Clare's little book, so slight and superficial,
served as a promptbook to help Joyce determine the incidents
of Bloom's day and Shakespeare's.

The character of Bloom could be solidified with such
materials, as well as with materials from Joyce's marital life.
For Stephen, Joyce had details of his premarital life available.
His mother's death, and his Paris sojourn, and his week in
Gogarty's tower, could be telescoped and made to cram

* Maurice Clare's own source was chiefly Thomas Fairman Ordish,
Shakespeare's London (London: Dent, 1904), which describes Gerard
at length, and also the Globe theatre and its bookstalls.

Stephen's mind. The main event of his own youth, his falling in love in June 1904, he assigned to Bloom, not Stephen, and dated sixteen years before the events of *Ulysses* are represented as taking place. Partly he was practising economy, and wanted to save the love life of his twenties for the Stephen-like Richard Rowan in *Exiles*. But partly he was resolved to keep Stephen's affective life as yet unrealized. This would make it easier for Stephen's mind and Bloom's eventually to jigsaw together. So Bloom exists more completely than Stephen in the sensory world, and Stephen more completely than Bloom in the intellectual one. If Bloom ponders physics, and takes them for constipation, Stephen is always having a dose of metaphysics. The attraction of Hamlet was that he too saw his own lot in philosophical terms, and required an outlet in thought as well as in action. Besides, as Wilhelm Meister had pointed out, Hamlet differs from most characters in plays because he retards the action, and in this way is especially suited to novels which depend less than do plays on swift action.

To thicken Stephen's consciousness, Joyce allowed himself to be prompted by two French writers, Mallarmé and Dujardin. Both had dealt with a young and self-conscious hero, in quite different ways. Mallarmé, in two essays which Joyce knew and quoted from, turned *Hamlet* into an internal drama. His Hamlet reads the book of himself, and the people he encounters are only metamorphoses of himself. So Laertes is his belligerence, Polonius his folly, and as for Ophelia, she is the virginity of his childhood. In effect, though Mallarmé never quite says so, Hamlet writes his own play, imposing his private dilemmas on the area about him which only seems to be an external world. Quite in keeping with this internal dramaturgy is what Mallarmé calls 'the sumptuous and stagnant exaggeration of murder', a phrase quoted by Stephen in support of his theory of the play's autobiographical configuration. The possibility of seeing reality as completely subjective is present to Stephen, who says that Shakespeare 'found in the world without as actual what was in his world within as possible'. But what he means, with Vico, is that anybody in some sense contains everybody, rather than, with Mallarmé, that no way out of the labyrinth of self exists.

Throughout the book Stephen deals with two philosophical problems; the first is whether the world has an objective existence, as maintained by Aristotle, or whether, as Hume considered, 'Nothing exists but subjective states, organized by the brute force of association. There is no self, no external world.' In the *Proteus* episode Stephen is firmly Aristotelean, and decides in favour of both an external world and a self. Six episodes later, in *Scylla and Charybdis*, the same questions arise and the same conclusions are reached, but less firmly. The mind is poised upon doubt as the world upon the void, Stephen concedes. After this Hume begins to have his innings. The dangers of selfhood manifest themselves in the *Cyclops* episode, in which the Citizen can see nothing but a nation-wide egoism, and in *Circe*, where seemingly external events of the day are whirled along concurrently with feelings into a nightmare orgy of self- and world-destruction, out of which the characters, and their world, finally re-emerge into separable identities. But neither world nor self seems so solid afterwards as it did before being melted down in Bella Cohen's brothel.

The other French book which awoke Joyce to new possibilities was Edouard Dujardin's small volume, *Les Lauriers sont coupés*. Joyce had happened on it in a newspaper kiosk in 1902 or 1903. The book, originally published in 1889, was for a long time forgotten, and it is in fact eminently forgettable; but Joyce's memory was democratic and he remembered it well. During the First World War he wrote to Dujardin from Zurich asking if he could possibly send him a copy, none being available in Switzerland and his own being locked up in Trieste. Although Joyce tipped off Larbaud to the importance of this book in his own career, *Les Lauriers* has seemed to some critics too inferior a work to be given so much credit. But if Dujardin was not a great novelist, he had good ideas for novels. He begins with a young hero who is soliloquizing, and the whole book is a soliloquy. The technique, later known as the internal monologue, makes for some clumsiness when the hero has to describe

outer circumstances, and Joyce had to refine Dujardin a good
deal to make him workable. But what initially captured his
attention, I think, was something else, that on the very first
page the young man performs a strange act – he invokes himself
into being. In the midst of random circumstance he surges into
identity:

> Car sous le chaos des apparences, parmi les durées et les sites,
> dans l'illusion des choses qui s'engendrent et qui s'enfantent, un
> parmi les autres, un commes les autres, distinct des autres, semblable
> aux autres, un le même et un de plus, de l'infini des possibles
> existences, je surgis: et voici que le temps et lieu se précisent; c'est
> l'aujourd'hui; c'est d'ici; l'heure qui sonne; et autour de moi, la
> vie. . . .*

As though to prove that this paragraph was no accident,
Dujardin's hero returns to it near the book's end, this time to
say that he has created in himself this day and hour, this *here*,
wherein life, or his dream of life, manifest themselves in place
and time as crystallized by a particular woman. He is his own
Prospero. The philosophy may be amateurish, but in arguing
the case of subjectivity against objectivity it anticipates Joyce's
fictional uses of philosophy. It domesticates metaphysics.

Dujardin's hero claims a place in the sun, but under the
moon his philosophy dwindles and he is bamboozled by his
mistress. Though no rival for her affections is ever given shape,
it seems clear that there is one, and that he is successful. The
protagonist joins that memorable group of Charles Bovary, the
hero of Paul de Kock's *Le Cocu*, and other cuckolds in whom
Joyce showed exceptional interest. In his notes to *Exiles*, Joyce
remarked that modern interest in stories of cuckoldry had
shifted from the lover to the betrayed husband. Dujardin
dwelt upon the victim almost exclusively. His half-expressed

* 'For, from beneath the chaos of appearances, from among the
stretches of time and space, amid the illusion of things that beget
and bear themselves, one among many, one like the others, unlike
the others, resembling the others, the same yet one more, out of the
infinity of possible lives, I arise: so time and place come to a point;
it is this day, it is here; this hour that is striking; and all around me
life . . .'

thoughts were appropriate for Bloom, but they could also be developed for Stephen. The latter profits a good deal. Not only does he admonish himself, 'Hold to the now, the here', but he also considers more professionally the problem posed amateurishly by Dujardin's hero, the relation of individual existence to space and time, the degree to which the world we see is simply our shadow. Hamlet, though he scoffed at philosophy, had faced this problem too, as is indicated by his bewailing that time is out of joint, and declaring he would be king of infinite space were it not that he had bad dreams. The sense of being at odds with the prevailing categories of perception, yet subject to them, perplexes Stephen.

4 *Spacetime*

Joyce needed in his book an element that would correspond to the sense the Greeks possessed, of preterhuman forces governing human life. In the *Odyssey* the influence came from Olympus, where the gods were real, or almost real, and not simply counters. Joyce found in space and time powers as elemental as Neptune and Hyperion, but secularized. Our lives are on the one hand enforced movements from room to room, concessions to our surroundings. On the other hand, our lives are enforced surrenders to tick and tock, temporal exigencies which wear us down whether we like it or not. We are creatures of our maps, and of our watches. When T. S. Eliot writes, 'Teach us to sit still', or speaks of 'the still point of the turning world', he seeks freedom from these mundane powers. But where Eliot looks for a relief which is institutionally covenanted, Joyce finds a possibility of relief in secular terms. We free ourselves from time and space, from history and geography, by memory, which fables itself into art.

Stephen Dedalus has to wait till the beginning of the third chapter to be alone, and once alone, he immediately follows the example of Dujardin's hero in launching into a meditation on space and time and their relation to the self. After conceding their ineluctableness, he tries to elude them. In the space world he shuts his eyes, in the time world he opens them. Space and time keep their hold: 'There all the time without you: and ever shall be, world without end.' Yet rumours of their overthrow pervade the book: the world they appear to rule may be only provisionally real, or it may be made of imaginative stuff rather than of matter. (Stephen has read Berkeley.) Even before he had named the rulers of the world in the third chapter, Stephen in the second chapter had imagined their annihilation: 'I hear the ruin of all space, shattered glass and toppling masonry, and time one livid final flame.'

In the second half of the book, these premonitions begin to be realized. Time and space, once so firm and masterful, begin to crumble, and both continuity and contiguity are repudiated. The bonds that keep things next to or before and after each other are loosened, objects and creatures appear from nowhere and events that should be prior are subsequent and otherwise disarranged. In the *Circe* episode the ruin of time and space is like a frame embracing the events: at the beginning Stephen is represented as raising his stick and shattering the lampshade, like a dumbshow of what is to follow at the episode's end, when with his stick, which he rechristens *Nothung*, he commits this destructive-creative act. What has been prefigured occurs: the stage direction reads, 'Time's livid final flame leaps, and, in the following darkness, ruin of all space, shattered glass and toppling masonry.' That which he envisaged in the mind's eye in Chapter II is effected symbolically by his own hand in Chapter XV. This ritual defiance of space and time is Stephen's defiance of the powers that govern the world; that he should be their defier is appropriate, for art has always claimed supremacy by making 'one little world an everywhere'. In blunt paraphrase, the mind is its own space and time, though it was Satan who said so, and the true plenitude of the world appears when, its gods put down, it appears most impoverished.

In portraying this larger struggle, the flouting of the *données* of perception, Joyce drew heavily upon *Hamlet*. The misery of Stephen at the corruption of his island has an analogue in the rot of Denmark as well as of Ithaca. Things rank and gross in nature possess the countries utterly. Corruption affects the family: 'Houses of decay,' Stephen thinks, 'mine, his, and all.' He berates himself for inability to save a man from drowning, as Hamlet berates himself for having failed to save Ophelia from a like fate. Stephen's image of the corpse fished out of the sea is also like Hamlet's meditation on Yorick, which finds several echoes as well in Bloom's thoughts at Glasnevin.

As if to balance the way that *Hamlet* throws into question the theatrical conventions by staging a play within a play, one fiction doubling another, Joyce makes Stephen's soliloquy question the basis of soliloquy, by exploring the twin perils that the world may be insubstantial, and he equally so. He tests the reality of the world by seeing whether it depends for existence upon being seen, or more precisely, upon being 'thought through my eyes'. If he closes his eyes, he can still feel it beneath his feet, or hit his head against it. Can he then think it away? No, it defies his would-be solipsism. He tests the reality of his self by pondering a debt he owes to George Russell. If his self is physical only, then the fact that his body cells have all changed since the debt was contracted means that he is no longer liable for it. If his self is spiritual only, then material obligations have no existence. Stephen is obliged to concede that his self is psychophysical, so that the debt, like the world in which it was contracted, cannot be thought away. He rejects both materialism and etherealism.

The book as a whole, also, besides Stephen within it, addresses itself to the validity of egoistic selfhood, as epitomized by the adversaries Mulligan, Boylan, the Cyclops, the narrator Thersites, and slowly but surely rejects it. Bloom, with his advocacy of love, tries to put out the Citizen's Cyclopean 'I'. Stephen joins in with his analogical argument, that as God is in all of us, so is the artist, and by extension, all are in all. In this sense art does hold the mirror up to nature, and can only second a sociability that nature has initiated.

The problem of the origin of art becomes a problem of the nature of man, and therefore has to be solved in the book. Joyce writes *Ulysses* with an eye to symbology similar to that which Yeats devised in *A Vision* and in many poems. For Yeats the voyage to Byzantium is the purging of the soul in death, but it is also the purging of daytime images in the midnight of the artist's imagination. For Joyce the development of his book is not only a movement towards the solution of his characters' knots, it is also a record of the creative process. From this point of view the fourteen episodes before *Circe* patiently accumulate the materials which in *Circe* are set into cerebral whirling and emerge in crystallizations like artistic offspring.

5   *Cerebral Mating*

Underlying Joyce's apprehension of art is the thesis that it is natural to be an artist. He agreed with Carlyle's idea in 'The Hero as Poet' that the artistic character is universal: 'A vein of poetry exists in the hearts of all men; no man is made altogether of Poetry. . . . A man that has so much more of the poetic element developed in him as to have become noticeable, will be called Poet by his neighbours.' Joyce wished his book to make this clear. If 'there's a touch of the artist about old Bloom', he is not alone in this. In his early essay, 'Drama and Life', Joyce contended that drama was 'mere animal instinct applied to the mind', and what he appears to have meant, even then, was that the artistic process mimics the natural process of reproduction. Just how this could be done was a subject he explored further in *Ulysses* than in his other writings. As soon as Bloom and Stephen begin to work in tandem, that is, from the *Aeolus* episode, Joyce calls attention to their joint aesthetic policy. In the newspaper office both assail the falsifications of ideals and the corruptions of language that empurple prose. But in *Lestrygonians* and *Scylla and Charybdis* Joyce makes clear, by Bloom's example and Stephen's precept, how the reproductive process of art works. In both he displays a process of coupling animal spirits with ethereal ones, facts with fancies, bodies with minds. Stephen in *Scylla and Charybdis* also finds the process to be one of joining treble and bass like woman and man. His theory leads him to claim for the artist androgyny. (Joyce had praised crusty Ibsen for his womanliness.) It also leads him to see the world without as in some sense the world within; our experiences seek us out because we want them to.

The copulatory image was a guarantee of naturalness, and the male and female elements could be varied as necessary. But Joyce wished to emphasize that the imagination did not float freely, but was anchored to remembered materials. He had first expressed in *Stephen Hero* (78) his view that the artist had to draw his images from his experience. In *Oxen of the Sun*, a chapter which appears to be about the birth of a baby in nature, but it is covertly also about the birth of a work of art, Joyce celebrates memory as a form of resurrection:

Francis was reminding Stephen of years before when they had been at school together in Conmee's time. He asked about Glaucon, Alcibiades, Pisistratus. Where were they now? Neither knew. You have spoken of the past and its phantoms, Stephen said. Why think of them? If I call them into life across the waters of Lethe will not the poor ghosts troop to my call? Who supposes it? I, Bous Stephanoumenos, bullockbefriending bard, am lord and giver of their life. He encircled his gadding hair with a coronal of vineleaves, smiling at Vincent. That answer and those leaves, Vincent said to him, will adorn you more fitly when something more, and greatly more, than a capful of light odes can call your genius father. All who wish you well hope this for you. All desire to see you bring forth the work you meditate. I heartily wish you may not fail them. O no, Vincent, Lenehan said, laying a hand on the shoulder near him, have no fear. He could not leave his mother an orphan. The young man's face grew dark. All could see how hard it was for him to be reminded of his promise and of his recent loss. (415; 543)

The dead can be reborn through the medium of art. Joyce had written Miss Weaver that the *Oxen of the Sun* was 'the most difficult episode in an odyssey, I think, both to interpret and to execute . . .' (I. 137). The difficulty came in making natural and artistic issue analogous to each other, yet in differentiating them as well. Joyce found a hint for a solution in the fact that the oxen which are sacred to the fertility god are themselves sterile. They might well serve as title for a chapter which praised the parturition of works of art but acknowledged that such progeny cannot move outside the page.

Joyce demonstrated the naturalness of the artistic process in the *Circe* episode which immediately follows the *Oxen of the Sun*. The ingredients of this episode are all phantoms of the past, memories recent or remote, and so eligible to become works of art. They do indeed become so at the end, when Stephen and Bloom independently summon phantoms across the waters of Lethe. But memories alone will not suffice, the imagination must ovulate a possible future for them, and in so doing, make possible an unforeseen blend of memory and imagination. At the end of *Circe*, they do indeed become the stuff of art, when Stephen and Bloom re-beget them. Stephen calls up the ghost of his dead mother, but out of his guilt and remorse, imaginatively brewed with love and pity, she takes on a harsh censoriousness and punitiveness that in life she did not have. The result is not May Dedalus as she was, but May Dedalus in a revised version of her marriage day, hideous with bridal veil over her dead face. Stephen's muse embitters his memory, and out of pity and terror he produces a figure from tragedy rather than comedy. Bloom's muse is kinder, allowing him to re-beget and re-conceive his son Rudy, who is then born from his head like Athena from the head of Zeus, but altered from the misshapen dwarflike creature who died at eleven days, and re-embodied as a perfect eleven-year-old boy, orthodox in religion as Bloom was not, a father's dream yet totally indifferent to that father. Bloom's memories have wedded with his aspirations, with his perceptions of Stephen, with his remorse for having begotten no living son and for having left the faith of his fathers. So remembered images penetrate the brain, there to be fertilized and passed through a process of gestation from which they emerge as new creatures. That they are new is proven by Mrs. Dedalus's unmaternal threats as by Rudy's unfilial indifference. Together they befit Joyce's conception of the artist – Shakespeare or another – as 'a deathsman of the soul' as well as a reanimator.

At this climactic moment Joyce, like Shakespeare, has two ghosts on stage, a parent and a child. Mrs. Dedalus is not so splendid as the majesty of buried Denmark, nor is Rudy so noble a heart as Horatio's 'sweet prince'. If neither Bloom nor Stephen is more than a crude Shakespeare, they are none the less artists, mixing memory and desire to bear artistic issue. The living Shakespeare evokes himself as dead man and his dead son Hamnet as living one; Stephen evokes his mother as dead woman and Bloom his son Rudy as living. This is Joyce's principal equivalent to the play within a play (there are joking playlets as well in Stephen's consciousness in the library scene); that is, it is his model for the artistic process which is at work within the book as a whole.

That both mother and child behave independently of their creators is because they are works of art, at least fragmentary, inchoate ones. They are no longer under control as the mother terrifies Stephen and the son ignores Bloom. The processes of mental life distort and refine the materials furnished by memory.

Whether the new work of art, when born, is to be described as an infant or an adult, is a problem that occurred to Joyce. With his usual thoroughness, he takes it up in two places. Stephen, knocked down by the soldiers, doubles himself up like a baby in the womb; Bloom lies down by Molly in the same posture, 'the childman weary, the manchild in the womb.' (Joyce seems to be considering the same idea when he gives Stephen, at the end of *A Portrait*, a spiritual birth to go with the physical birth he had at the beginning.) What Joyce implies in *Ulysses* is that just as parents look forth in the eyes of their children, so our ancestors, artistic and natural, look forth in us and in our works, whether these works are merely memories or more finished creations. He wished to show that *Ulysses* was at once a newborn babe and an ageold one, an experiment but also a thing done and completed. Literature is impregnated by life's memories; on the other hand, life's memories include those recalled from books. The fertile materials spill over everywhere. We are all in the process of remembering and reshaping in new form what we have encountered.

At this point Joyce's use of Homer and of Shakespeare becomes not a matter of finding archetypes for his characters, but of allowing them all to mingle in a sea of fiction and non-fiction. By force of individual passion, we body ourselves forth in human and artistic offspring. The interbreeding is constant. We are such stuff as dreams are made on and mortal tissue too. Shakespeare and Homer cease to be models and join a mammoth human family, a family in which works of art and people interchange, all begetting, bearing, being born. *Ulysses* at its outermost bound summons into existence *Finnegans Wake*, in which that total family is the material with which we begin rather than, as here, the material with which we end.

III

Joyce

1 *Aesthetics without Aesthetes*

During the period in Irish history when Joyce was coming of
age, the usual political gestures, such as voting in Parliamentary
elections, had no meaning. The word 'political', however, as
Roland Barthes says, describes 'the whole of human relations
in their real, social structure, in their power of making the
world.' Joyce is not often recognized as having functioned as a
political writer. The theory of art and its practice which is
usually drawn from his writings is that the artist is too Godlike
to take sides for or against his characters. Joyce, it is said, offers
instead multiple perspectives on the action, in the form of
different styles and different narrators, without choosing among
them. This is to malign God as well as Joyce. The view has
caught on a little because Flaubert sometimes expressed it, and
Joyce is held to be another Mauberley having Flaubert for his
true Penelope. Yet Flaubert's explicit statements about artistic
detachment are inadequate to explain *Madame Bovary*, where
the author, however unconfiding, describes the feelings of his
characters with an attentiveness that may be pokerfaced but is
not heartless. So much patient, detailed consideration hardly
jibes with the artist's being indifferent. Joyce exhibits this
attentiveness too, and with characters more obviously likable
than Flaubert's. Like Stephen, he accepts responsibility for
learning 'what the heart is and what it feels'. If he offers
multiple perspectives, his own view shows through, either
because a given perspective is obviously self-defeating, like that
of the sentimental narrator in the *Nausicaa* episode, or collides
with another, as with the opposed narrators of the *Cyclops*
episode. One always knows where Joyce is, even though he

never says. His true Penelope was not Flaubert: he was even captious about that master's allegedly perfect artistry, and dared to find fault with his choice of tenses. The writer Joyce did praise almost unreservedly was Tolstoy, who made no show of indifference at all. If, as Joyce wrote his daughter, 'How Much Land Does a Man Need?' is the finest of all short stories, it is so because of its sympathy for men in their follies. The quality for which Joyce praised people he admired was sincerity, for him the supreme virtue as well as the rarest. It was one he sought for himself, which he did not intend his elaborate means to conceal.

A second theory of art may be drawn from Joyce's writings. It has less to do with the qualities of the aesthetic object, its wholeness, harmony, and radiance, though these are not renounced. To think of artistry alone was for Joyce a mark of the aesthete rather than of the true artist; if Stephen is sometimes taken for an aesthete, that is a misunderstanding. An aesthete is what he is not. For Joyce Petrarch was an aesthete, and sometimes Yeats, insofar as he sought a beauty that was of the past. True beauty was, as Plato said, the splendour of truth, and truth required that there should be between the writer's life and his work an umbilical relation. The imagined and concocted were of no value beside the known and experienced; or, as Joyce said, the footprint Robinson Crusoe saw in the sand was worth more than the eternal city envisaged by St. John. The more genuine the urge to expression, the more it had to do with the most accessible feelings. Hence the impulse to drama, or indeed to all art, is coeval with life.

A classic statement of Joyce's programme comes at the end of *A Portrait of the Artist as a Young Man*. The peroration of Stephen's journal reads, in part, 'Welcome, O Life! . . .' Jaundiced critics have attempted to find an absurdity here, as if Joyce could write an exclamatory sentence only ironically. Of course Joyce was like Stephen aware that big words can make us unhappy, but he and his hero adopt the florid capital L for Life without fear. It does not matter that Stephen sounds more youthful here than in *Ulysses*: Joyce had a keen sense of the fervour and high spirits of youth, and Yeats remarked that in no one he had met, except William Morris, was the joy of life so keen as in Joyce. The Germans were enamoured of death, Joyce used to complain; his own persuasion was different. The whole of *A Portrait* prepared for an emotional release, and these words denote that Stephen is experiencing it. Nor was there irony in Stephen's following words, 'I go to encounter for the millionth time the reality of experience and to forge in the smithy of my soul the uncreated conscience of my race.' In the encounter with reality he is the millionth; in the forging of his race's conscience he acknowledges no predecessors. Although one astute critic, Edward Engelberg, construes conscience here as meaning consciousness, the artist's task being to bring the race to awareness of itself, Joyce used the word more plainly. By conscience he meant conscience, the creation of standards by which acts could be judged. By endowing Stephen with this mission, not suddenly but progressively throughout the book, he recognized the communal role of art.

This declaration on Stephen's part was one of those that Joyce allowed himself or his characters only at rare intervals. Another, which he made *in propria persona* as well as through Stephen, indicates that the purpose of the artistic conscience is to say yes rather than no. He first certified this function of art in his essay on James Clarence Mangan in 1902, where he held that the artist takes part 'in the continual affirmation of the spirit'. Shortly afterwards he has Stephen express the same view twice in *Stephen Hero*: 'Thus the spirit of man makes a continual affirmation . . .' (80), and 'The artist affirms out of the fulness of his own life . . .' (86). In *Ulysses* Stephen reiterates, this time to Bloom, 'the eternal affirmation of the spirit of man in literature'. Far from being inclined towards the position of the aesthete, Joyce has both Stephen and Bloom expressly disavow it, Stephen at the end of *A Portrait*, where he abjures retrospective beauty, and Bloom in *Lestrygonians* and *Sirens*, where he dismisses the 'creamy dreamy'. In the service of an ampler art, Joyce practised humility before the workings of the universe. No partial art, such as the aesthetes endorsed, could satisfy him, nor could any distillation of life, however refined, that ignored grossness.

For him the mind was profoundly physical, containing all the organs of the body. An art which failed to suggest that its characters were capable of defecating, urinating, masturbating, copulating, menstruating, was for Joyce a falsification. Bodiliness was a measure that could be applied to books as to lives. Having read *By the Stream at Killmeen*, a group of stories written by his Irish contemporary, Seamas O'Kelly, Joyce noted that they were 'about beautiful, pure faithful Connacht girls and lithe, broad-shouldered open-faced young Connacht men', and then concluded, as he wrote his brother, without anger, 'Well, there's no doubt they are very romantic young people: at first they come as a relief, then they tire. Maybe, begod, people like that are to be found by the Stream of Killmeen only none of them has come under my observation, as the deceased gent in Norway remarked' (II. 196). (Ibsen had just died.) To be sentimental was to deny the body, an offence just as serious as to deny the soul, and meant shirking responsibility by evasion. It was a form of Not-Life, an appeal to an old order which was not less vicious for that order's having never existed. As such, it was one form of self-blinding, which the newly forged conscience must prevent.

This conscience is communal, or racial as Joyce said. Dante hoped to bring his readers from the state of misery to one of felicity, and Joyce undertook such a venture too. Homer and Shakespeare may have had similar aims, but they show little sign of wishing to change the forms of society. Homer's Ulysses wishes, after all, to restore the *ancien régime* in Ithaca. Shakespeare's Ulysses (in *Troilus and Cressida*) defends degree as fervently as Bloom, following Dante, defends a love which passes all degree. Joyce was more radical than Homer or Shakespeare, the least willing to accept the world as he found it. That he considered this quality important is substantiated by a letter he wrote to his brother on 15 March 1905, at a time when he was establishing his character as artist: 'I believe that Ibsen and Hauptmann separate from the herd of writers because of their political aptitude – eh?' He had his own idea of how this aptitude might best be displayed.

2 Guerrilla Warfare

In the first draft of 'A Portrait of the Artist', which comes closer than any of his works to non-fictional autobiography, Joyce indicated that at one period in his development, he had been outspoken in his rebellion against institutions, specifically against the Church. 'But that outburst over,' he then writes, 'it was urbanity in warfare.' The term 'urbanity' is misleading, it suggests indulgence and tolerance, and its relation to 'warfare' is antithetical; a term less paradoxical would be 'obliquity'. This is the quality which shapes Joyce's treatment of institutions in all his works. It went with the distaste for didacticism, shared with Flaubert. Sometimes he is so oblique that he is believed in some quarters not to have been conducting warfare at all.

Apologists for his Catholicism have pointed out that he repudiates the Church in *A Portrait* only to the degree that it impinges upon his hero, and not absolutely. But that is merely to say that he keeps within the frame of his fiction; it does not reduce the authority of Stephen as a model. Joyce's attitude towards the State has also been misinterpreted, not least by Marxist critics. At the Congress of Writers in Kharkov in 1933, Karl Radek accused him of being a defender of bourgeois capitalism, and some non-Marxist critics, reading *Ulysses* the same way, have marvelled at what they take to be Joyce's complacency about the social order, or what Lionel Trilling has called his indifference to politics. Still, the author of *Dubliners* could scarcely be considered complacent, and the misconstrual arises from his indirectness. S. L. Goldberg has lamented that Joyce failed in *Ulysses* to display the evils of modern industrialism as D. H. Lawrence in *Women in Love* exposed the horrors of the coal mines. There would in fact be a difficulty in placing coal mines in an Irish setting. (Mr. Goldberg concedes this point.) Yet Joyce was not altogether at a loss because of the lack of heavy industry in his country. He used instead as his principal emblem of modern capitalism the newspaper, wasting the spirit with its persistent attacks upon the integrity of the word, narcotizing its readers with superficial facts, habituating them to secular and clerical authority. Even here Joyce's attack is oblique, but it is not indulgent, not tolerant, not indifferent. His obliquity was in the service of a point of view, an idea.

At the start of his career, he all but gave the idea a name. In the same draft, 'A Portrait of the Artist', he concluded in a cryptic manner, 'Already the messages of citizens were flashing along the wires of the world, already the generous idea had emerged from a thirty years' war in Germany and was directing the councils of the Latins.' The generous idea was socialism, not particularized as to school; by the 'thirty years' war in Germany' he may have meant the period after the Gotha agreement of 1875 when the socialist factions agreed to work together, and by the 'councils of the Latins' he must have meant the socialist parties in the Latin countries. Not naming socialism except as 'the generous idea' was probably part of that obliquity upon which he had set himself.

But at the close of this essay he makes another of his eloquent perorations: 'To these multitudes, not as yet in the womb of humanity but surely engenderable there, he would give the word: Man and woman, out of you comes the nation that is to come, the lightening of your masses in travail, the competitive order is arrayed against itself, the aristocracies are supplanted, and amid the general paralysis of an insane society, the confederate will issues in action.' The tone, if not the purport, is like that of other manifestoes, including the Communist one. He seems to agree with Marx that capitalism bears within itself its own destruction, and that aristocracies must go. The confederate will seems to mean the will of likeminded revolutionaries. Like W. H. Auden, Joyce conceives of the Just as sending out their messages across national boundaries, and imagines them as conspiratorially united, though he avoids those words, 'confederate' being an oblique form of them.

His own function was that of a sentry sounding an alarm, in the name of what in *Stephen Hero* he called 'a new humanity, active, unafraid and unashamed'. As he said there,

He wished to express his nature freely and fully for the benefit of a society which he would enrich and also for his own benefit, seeing that it was part of his life to do so. It was not part of his life to attempt an extensive alteration of society but he felt the need to express himself such an urgent need, such a real need, that he was determined no conventions of a society, however plausibly mingling pity with its tyranny should be allowed to stand in his way, and though a taste for elegance and detail unfitted him for the part of a demagogue, from his general attitude he might have been supposed not unjustly an ally of the collectivist politicians, who are often very seriously upbraided by opponents who believe in Jehovahs, and decalogues and judgments with sacrificing the reality to an abstraction. (146–7)

'Supposed not unjustly an ally of the collectivist politicians': the double negative may be oblique but its meaning is clear.

By the time Joyce rephrased this in the completed *A Portrait of the Artist as a Young Man*, it had become the question: 'How could he hit their conscience or how cast his shadow over the imaginations of their daughters, before their squires begat upon them that they might breed a race less ignoble than their own?' To catch the conscience of the people in his book must be his motive. Literature is a revolutionary instrument, however roundabout it may move.

Ulysses is in fact, as I have intimated, Joyce's Trojan horse: a monument, but full of armed men; a comedy, but with teeth and claws. Stephen's insistence upon reconsidering time and space has another purpose besides the extolling of art's independence of these categories. It is political as well. For Stephen associates space with body and time with soul; the one is visible, the other invisible. He thereby relates them to the servitudes he has acknowledged in the first chapter of *Ulysses*: 'I am the servant of two masters. . . . The Imperial British state . . . and the holy Roman apostolic church.' There is also a third, he says, who wants him for odd jobs – mother Ireland, herself the servant of a servant. The secular and spiritual powers, visible and invisible worlds, are equally extortionate. 'Are not Religion and Politics the same thing?' asks Blake in *Jerusalem* (III, 657). Stephen allies himself with another conviction of Blake, that 'the king and the priest must be tied in a tether'. Stanislaus reports in *My Brother's Keeper* (154) that Joyce was fond of quoting this line before he left Dublin. As Blake said in his commentary on Dante, we must 'go into the mind in which everyone is king and priest in his own house', and Yeats, in *Ideas of Good and Evil*, which Joyce had with him in Trieste, explained that 'The phrase about the king and priest is a memory of the crown and mitre set upon Dante's head before he entered Paradise.' The passage in Canto 27 of the *Purgatorio* (*'io te sopra te corono e mitrio'*) was then much in Joyce's mind, and he used it for symbolic effect as his predecessors had done. The priest lays claim to an eternity of time, as the king if he could would rule over infinite space; and against these forces, anthropomorphized in earthly authorities, Stephen and Bloom have to muster their own forces.

Ulysses provides a measure against which British State and Catholic Church can be evaluated, and Ireland as well, both in its patent collusion with these forces, and in the callousness which the desire for independence could evoke. If British tyranny was brutally materialistic, so was Irish fanaticism. Persecution, by Church or by State, whether of Jews or of artists, went with other forms of materialism, such as sexual cruelty and lovelessness. On the other side was an etherealism which included the diseased ideals of religion and patriotism, ideals without body and essences without form, antisexualism or love cheapened by sentimentality. The statues of Nelson and Moses, evoked in the newspaper episode, symbolize the two poles, while Parnell, whose image in the cabman's shelter seems equally false ('Dead he wasn't. Simply absconded somewhere'), is the local focus for political extravagance and violence.

What Joyce does is to bring pressure to bear at different points and with different degrees of intensity. It would have been possible for him to sharpen his pen by representing as ogres both Father Conmee, as a high functionary of the Church, and the Viceroy as the chief representative of the State. But he is careful not to do that. The Viceroy and Father Conmee, who traverse Dublin emblematically in the *Wandering Rocks* episode, are allowed to be personally inoffensive. Even the Cyclops, as Irish chauvinist, has a turn of phrase, though it's a wrong turn, and likes his dog, though it turns out to be somebody else's. Yet each is obliquely repudiated. Benevolent Father Conmee has no sense of the strength or value of the appetites he seeks to repress, nor of the rigidity of the Church which he serves so devotedly. But Bloom and Stephen, each in his own way, remark its sado-masochistic elements, and Stephen especially sees it as a nightmare preying upon the living. As for the Viceroy, Joyce represents him mildly enough as on his way to a charity benefit. The clatter and ringing of the viceregal carriage are grand. On the other hand, it is viceregal spies who report on the native populace to the Castle, and the viceregal soldiers who bully Stephen. Bloom, hearing the phrase, 'Our lovely land', asks with a pertinence which is emphasized, 'Whose land?' He fully supports Irish independence, but he challenges the Citizen on the use of force, and has to endure the Citizen's attempt to use force against him. He challenges etherealism, too, in a small way by refusing to see a newspaper publisher as 'the image of our Saviour', in a larger one by shrewdly anatomizing the rites of confession, communion, and extreme unction, by rejecting chastity, by repudiating the false idealization of both woman and of country.

Stephen is equally unwilling to accept the occupying authority, and he too has this for one of his targets. He savagely mocks both British glories and Irish chauvinism with his Parable of the Plums spat out upon Ireland's promised land from Nelson's pillar. Like Bloom, he repudiates the use of force to achieve independence, so will have nothing to do with Old Gummy Granny who offers him the glorious opportunity of dying in armed struggle for Ireland. After a booklong attack upon the etherealism of Dublin rhetoric, whether in the service of piety or patriotism, Stephen combats materialism when he tells Private Carr that he must kill the priest and king in his own mind, a political remark for which he is promptly knocked down.

3 *Political Antecedents*

The attack on space and time, then, is elaborately coordinated with an attack upon the visible and invisible authorities in Ireland. The attempt to destroy space and time through art becomes a similitude of the attempt to overcome State and Church through language, by rendering them ridiculous, by disclosing their secret natures, by flouting them directly and indirectly. Joyce's political awareness was based on considerable reading. His library in Trieste included especially books by socialists and anarchists. He had, for example, the first 173 Fabian tracts bound in one volume. Among other writers who interested him were notably the two anarchists, Kropotkin and Bakunin, and the social reformer, Proudhon.

Peter Kropotkin's pamphlet on *Anarchist Morality* denied any validity to the old dichotomy of egoism and altruism, on the ground that, willynilly, people's interests are mutual. Kropotkin might be borrowing from Joyce, rather than Joyce from Kropotkin, when he declares, 'the condition of the maintenance of life is its expansion'. Joyce read Proudhon's *Qu'est-ce que la propriété?* with equal attention. Proudhon defines slavery as murder and property as theft. His views appear to underlie the discussion in *Exiles* of robbery. Little Archie asks his father, Richard Rowan, whether there are robbers in Ireland as in Rome, and receives the reply, 'There are poor people everywhere.' Richard then goes on to ask, 'Do you know what it is to give? . . . While you have a thing it can be taken from you. . . . But when you give it, you have given it. No robber can take it from you. . . . It will be yours always. That is to give.' Richard in the play tries to apply this principle to love as well as to money. When Proudhon quotes an old definition of trade as the 'art of buying for three francs what is worth six, and of selling for six what is worth three', he might be priming Stephen to reply to Mr. Deasy's attack on Jewish businessmen, 'A merchant is one who buys cheap and sells dear, jew or gentile, is he not?' Proudhon's injunction, 'Speak without hate or fear: say what you know', is also in the Joycean manner. 'On then: dare it', Stephen tells himself. These radical reformers fascinated Joyce by the sweep and finality of their writings as well as by their subversiveness.

His principal political authority was, I think, Bakunin, whose *God and the State* (London: Freedom Press, 1910, translated by the anarchist Benjamin Tucker, himself one of Joyce's admirations) examined the relation between certain philosophical and political concepts in a way Joyce could put to use. Bakunin condemned on the other hand a brutal materialism, and on the other its seeming opposite, a lofty idealism; to both, he pointed out, *matter* was vile, a representation of 'supreme nothingness'. Joyce could take advantage of this hint by displaying the collusion between the brutal materialism of Buck Mulligan, his indifference to the consequences of his acts and words, and the mysticism of George Russell, for whom acts done in this world are merely lying semblances. Bakunin connects the materialism of the State with the idealism of the Church, and sees them both as united in the enslavement of humanity. 'All religions are cruel, all founded on blood,' he declares, and concludes that all religions 'rest principally on the idea of sacrifice, that is, on the perpetual immolation of humanity to the insatiable vengeance of divinity.' Bloom concurs: 'God wants blood victim. Birth, hymen, martyr, war, foundation of a building, sacrifice, kidney, burnt-offering, druid's altars.' During the day both he and Stephen delineate the bloodthirstiness of Church and State, their cruelty and their urge to flatten out individual freedoms.

While Bloom's remarks, though a little muddled ('foundation of a building' does not fit in so well), are close to Bakunin's in their expression, Stephen is allowed by Joyce to put his own view more gnomically. So in Nighttown Stephen tells the soldier Carr, 'You die for your country, suppose. But I say, let

my country die for me. Up to the present it has done so. I
don't want it to die.' He is a little drunk, but he means that
sacrifice can enslave as well as free. The purpose of nationalism
is the expansion of life, not its abbreviation. Later Stephen
remarks somewhat testily to Bloom, 'You think I am important
because I belong to the Faubourg Saint Patrice called Ireland
for short. But I think Ireland is important because it belongs to
me.' The State is the instrument of its members, not their
enslaver.

Notwithstanding such bursts of impatience, Stephen keeps in
Ulysses as in *A Portrait* a basic loyalty to his country, and
repudiates those who, as he shrewdly conjectures of Mulligan,
will betray it. Whatever tendency Stephen has to wash his
hands of Ireland, he cannot be anti-Irish for long. So at the
end of *A Portrait*, having devoted one entry in his journal to
mocking the Irish mentality, he comes to the conclusion, 'Then
into Nile mud with it!' But in his next entry he rebukes himself
with the words, 'Disapprove of this last phrase.' In *Ulysses* he
recognizes his kinship with even the grossest of his compatriots,
'Their blood is in me, their lusts my waves.' One of his most
pro-Irish statements is unreported and has to be inferred from
a remark which his music teacher makes in reply to something
Stephen has just said. The teacher says in Italian, 'I once had the
same ideas when like you I was young. But then I became con-
vinced that the world was a beast.' What Stephen has just said,
discreetly omitted by Joyce as too close to the knuckle, is that
he intends to write for the benefit of his race; Artifoni's reply
only shows that he has fallen into the idealist error of treating
the world as vile.

Since they anatomize and deride Church and State alike,
Bloom and Stephen might be supposed to be anarchists. Joyce
has sometimes been linked to this point of view, too. He did
maintain a lifelong interest in anarchism, and once, in a poem
he wrote in Zurich, 'Dooleysprudence', he expressed anarchist
views in music hall terms:

Who is the funny fellow who declines to go to church
Since pope and priest and parson left the poor man in the lurch

And taught their flocks the only way to save all human souls
Was piercing human bodies through with dumdum bulletholes?
    It's Mr Dooley,
    Mr Dooley,
    The mildest man our country ever knew
    'Who will release us
    From Jingo Jesus'
    Prays Mr Dooley-ooley-ooley-oo.

      .   .   .   .   .

Who is the tranquil gentleman who won't salute the State
Or serve Nabuchodonesor or proletariat
But thinks that every son of man has quite enough to do
To paddle down the stream of life his personal canoe?
    It's Mr Dooley,
    Mr Dooley,
    The wisest wight our country ever knew
    'Poor Europe ambles
    Like sheep to shambles'
    Sighs Mr Dooley-ooley-ooley-oo.

Yet paddling his own canoe is not the policy of either Bloom or
Stephen, nor, whatever his reticence in Switzerland and Paris
about his politics, can it have been Joyce's. While neither
Bloom nor Stephen offers a coherent programme of change,
neither is satisfied with simply laying bare the inadequacies of
Irish spiritual and secular governors. Stephen is bent upon
affirming, and needling his compatriots into affirming, the
disused possibilities of life. He wants them to walk untrammelled
by petrified dogmas. For Bloom what is truly life is love,
possibly a crude term for his sense of mutuality of concern but
at least a traditional one. As a young man he was a socialist,
and annoyed Molly during their early acquaintance by in-
forming her that Christ was the first socialist. The Church he
finds bloodthirsty and prone to make victims, the State the
same. He has vague humanitarian goals. 'From each according
to his ability, to each according to his needs' becomes in his
version, 'To everyone according to his needs, and to everyone
according to his deeds.' On this plane Bloom appears ludicrous,
and Bloomusalem is an appropriate emblem for his Utopian
hopes of social regeneration. But clearly Joyce is here exag-

gerating to the point of absurdity Bloom's kindness and good-hearted civic feeling.

4 *Beyond Parnell*

Bloom's politics do not stop here. If his ultimate goals are (like most people's) indistinct, he has an immediate one that he understands very well. For what it is we have to look at the final chapter. Since Molly Bloom is apolitical herself, her monologue is not the place we would expect to find political information. But she is distressfully aware that her husband has views. They are likely to get him into trouble, she feels. She mentions them, in fact she cannot help mentioning them both early and late in her monologue. Even during their courtship Bloom was for Home Rule and the Land League. She complains, 'he was going about with some of them Sinner Fein lately or whatever they call themselves talking his usual trash and nonsense he says that little man he showed me without the neck is very intelligent the coming man Griffith is he well he doesnt look it thats all I can say still it must have been him he knew there was a boycott . . .' (784; 886). She is leery of her husband's losing his job with the *Freeman's Journal*: 'well have him coming home with the sack soon out of the Freeman too like the rest on account of those Sinner Fein or the Freemasons then well see if the little man he showed me dribbling along in the wet all by himself round by Coadys Lane will give him much consolation that he says is so capable and sincerely Irish he is indeed judging by the sincerity of the trousers I saw on him . . .' (772; 918). These references are insistent enough.

Joyce is sometimes said to have had no politics except regret for Parnell, yet he was not the man to worship the dead. For a long time now he had had his eye on a living leader, Arthur Griffith. Griffith, eleven years older than Joyce, had after some years of preliminary work founded in October 1902 the separatist organization which in 1905 was christened Sinn

Féin (Ourselves Alone). (Molly Bloom anticipates by sixteen months the later name.) His principal coadjutor had been William Rooney, a patriotic poet, who had died in 1901 at the age of twenty-eight. In 1902 Griffith published Rooney's poems, and it fell to Joyce to review them for the Unionist *Daily Express* (for which Gabriel in 'The Dead' also writes). The review attacked the poems first for being derivative, but more importantly, for being 'full of tears and curses'. 'And yet he might have written well if he had not suffered from one of those big words which make us so unhappy.' Griffith for answer quoted most of the review in an advertisement in his own newspaper, the *United Irishman*, and after 'big words' added '[Patriotism]'. It was a stroke Joyce could admire, even if aimed against himself.

He followed Griffith's subsequent activities closely, and in 1906 he made up his mind. A letter to his brother asserted flatly that a recent speech in Dublin by Griffith had justified the existence of his newspaper. In this speech Griffith advocated the boycott of English goods that Molly mentions, and also an educational system, a national banking system and a national civil service. He agreed with Bloom, and with Joyce, in not being a 'physical force' man.

Although he refused to endorse the revival of the Irish language, Joyce was in other ways on the side of the separatist movement, and particularly of Griffith's programme. He thought that the time for parliamentary action, of the sort espoused by Parnell, was over, and that an economic boycott would have more hope of succeeding. Of course the fanaticism of the extreme Sinn Féiners did not attract him, and he satirizes it in the Citizen, whose battle cry, *Sinn Féin amhain* ('Ourselves Alone for ever'), serves as a stick to beat anyone he doesn't like. Stephen also speaks of the 'archons of *Sinn Féin*' as giving Socrates his noggin of hemlock. But if Joyce did not like the extremist wing of the party, he approved Griffith's moderate programme.

He had personal and literary reasons as well for admiring Griffith. In 1911, when Joyce addressed a public letter to newspapers in Ireland about the suppression of *Dubliners*, most of the newspaper editors ignored it, only two published it, and of these two only Griffith risked libel action by publishing it in full. The next year, when Joyce was in Dublin, he asked and received Griffith's help for *Dubliners*, this time against the pseudo-nationalist machinations of an Irish publisher. From what he writes of his conversation with Griffith, he evidently won his help by insisting that his literary purpose was 'the spiritual liberation of my country' (a phrase he used to Grant Richards on 20 May 1906) – *Dubliners* was not a summons to action, yet it exposed the shortcomings of Irish life under British rule. He also pointed out that he was the only Irishman on the Adriatic coast writing articles for Home Rule in Triestine newspapers. On this trip, too, he acquired two of Griffith's recent pamphlets on the Home Rule bill then under parliamentary debate.

In *Ulysses* Joyce was encouraged by Bloom's Hungarian origin to relate him to Griffith's programme. Martin Cunningham says Bloom gave Griffith the idea of the Hungarian system, that is, of a dual monarchy for England and Ireland, on the model of the Austro-Hungarian empire. For much of his life Griffith espoused it, but the Easter Rising of 1916 made such a compromise impossible. Now total independence became his goal. He kept in the forefront of political activity, and in 1921 when the Irish Free State was in process of being created, he took a principal role. More to the point, for Joyce, was that on 8 January 1922 Arthur Griffith was elected first president of Ireland.

This was just the moment when Joyce was completing *Ulysses*, a coincidence he could not and did not resist. The references to Griffith in his final chapter are more than coincidence; Joyce wished to salute Griffith's at last successful efforts. Bloom is described as having once picked up Parnell's hat and handed it back to him, a homely gesture more attractive than rhetorical ones. Joyce offers Griffith, through the unwitting agency of Molly, a backhanded tribute, homely too. It was Griffith's programme, and not Parnell's, which had eventually won through. Ireland was achieving independence just as *Ulysses* was achieving publication. The political emancipation of Ireland had been accomplished by his old ally Griffith, and the emancipation of its conscience – Joyce's own lifetime work – was also approaching culmination. Bloom's sometime socialism, and Joyce's sometime socialism and anarchism, are put behind in order to hail, in Joyce's own fashion, the new country and the political leader to whom he felt most closely allied.

Ultimately *Ulysses* too constituted a political act, in the oblique fashion that Joyce used to express himself. Its humour was not offhand but a means of comic exploration of the shortcomings of life in Ireland as lived under British and Catholic authorities. To those who lived meaninglessly in a brutal and consuming present, Joyce offered a world of accountability and did not shrink from calling it spiritual. To those who, nursed by locally distorted Catholic doctrines, spoke of spiritual realities as if they alone existed, he pointed to the realities of the body's life. Like Dante he felt empowered to confer mitre and crown, a new politics of mind and body. That *Ulysses* like the Free State could come to exist was a major blow against those who wished to envisage life in a narrower style than it sponsored. The book summons into being a society capable of reading and enjoying it because capable of as frank and open an outlook on life as the book manifests. *Ulysses* creates new Irishmen to live in Arthur Griffith's new state.

For Joyce the creation of the Irish Free State was the culmination of his hopes. After 1922, the complexities that came with it interested him, and he followed them as he could from across the Channel. He mentions those who came after Griffith, De Valera in particular. The tergiversations of the Irish parties understandably did not arouse him to any strong partisanship. By this time, the political awareness demonstrated by his book made lesser manoeuvres redundant. On the other hand, the international situation pressed in upon him more and more. Joyce did not sign protests, and maintained his aloofness from all particular events except one, the Nazi butchery of the Jews.

On this point – which was the touchstone of politics in the
1930s – he did what he could, and by means of his intercession
perhaps a dozen people were aided to escape from Germany.
Such assistance meant more than many protests, and the idea
of personal help pleased him best as his scepticism of institutions
mounted.

5   *The Politics of Aesthetics*

Joyce's politics and aesthetics were one. For him the act of
writing was also, and indissolubly, an act of liberating. His
book examines the servitude of his countrymen to their masters
in Church and State, and offers an ampler vision. While the
criticism is severe, its aim is to unite rather than disunite. The
central action of *Ulysses* is to bring together Stephen Dedalus
and Leopold Bloom by displaying their underlying agreement
on political views which the author thereby underwrites. The
agreement is countersigned by Bloom's rescue of Stephen from
army and police after the young man has mentally defied both
Church and State.* That the two men converge only partially
does not diminish the exemplary value of their partial convergence. For a moment Bloom and Stephen, coming from the
two ends of the alphabet, can become Blephen and Stoom.

So the pun on names is also a pun about existence, and the
pun is Joyce's stock in trade beyond what is generally acknowledged. In a pun the component parts remain distinguishable,
and yet there is a constant small excitement in their being
yoked together so deftly and so improperly. An equivalence is
at once asserted and questioned, sounds and senses in mutual
trespass are both compared and contrasted. Puns are of

---

* Martin Cunningham and Joe Hynes assist in rescuing Bloom from
the Citizen, as Corny Kelleher assists in rescuing Stephen from the
Watch (police). Their cooperation is less momentous than Bloom's
Good Samaritan act, but suggests that Dublin is not devoid of
compassion or good will.

different kinds, and their effects are also various, so that they make us laugh or wince, are random or substantive, conjure up lofty associations or vulgar ones. Words are expatriated and repatriated like Dubliners. Joyce exploited all these nuances, and the pun becomes the key to his work – a key both aesthetic and political, both linguistic and moral.

The pun extends beyond words. The same process goes on with people and incidents. A law of the Joycean universe is that every single thing is always on the verge of doubling with another. Doubling reaches a nightmare pitch in *Circe*, when Bella becomes Bello, when Bloom doubles as Henry Flower and also as a woman, and when wallpaper and pictures assume human voices. But similar events occur throughout the book: Paddy Dignam is dead, yet several people believe they have seen him or his ghost; that 'the ghost walks' means that the paymaster on the newspaper is making his rounds, as well as that the majesty of buried Denmark walks the night along with the sepulchral wraith of May Dedalus. Bloom meets a sailor who calls himself Murphy but appears to be a mock Bloom, just as he meets M'Coy whose wife, like his own, is a soprano. In Molly Bloom's mind Mulvey on the Rock of Gibraltar doubles with Bloom on the Hill of Howth. The characters also tend to double with mythical archetypes, divine and human. The implications of the meeting of Bloom and Stephen, their connections with Ulysses and Telemachus, with King Hamlet and Prince Hamlet, with Shakespeare and Hamnet, are infinitely extensible. To the complaint that they do not fuse Joyce would doubtless have answered that the essence of the pun is not complete but incomplete juncture. To have them fuse would be to abolish the reason for their having been brought together. The parts of the pun keep their identities even while these are demonstrated to be less isolating than they appeared. And the resemblances between two men, and two sounds, are themselves made up of further resemblances to other people and other sounds.

That is why the word 'metempsychosis' is mentioned so prominently in the first scene between Bloom and his wife. She wants to know what it means, and he endeavours not too successfully to explain it to her.* The spirit of one word enters another, as the spirit of one situation, or of one being. The pun is metempsychosis. Whole areas of thought, as well as small knots of words, prove to be fluid rather than solid. In one of his letters, Joyce takes up a nine-word sentence in *Finnegans Wake* (104), and finds seven meanings flowing through it:

L'Arcs en His Cieling Flee Chinx on the Flur.
1) God's in his heaven All's Right with the World
2) The Rainbow is in the sky (arc-en-ciel) the Chinese (Chinks) live tranquilly on the Chinese meadowplane (China alone almost of the old continent[s] has no record of a Deluge. Flur in this sense is German. It suggests also Flut (flood) and Fluss (river) and could even be used poetically for the expanse of a waterflood. Flee = free)
3) The ceiling of his (ⵎ) house is in ruins for you can see the birds flying and the floor is full of cracks which you had better avoid

---

* I suspect that Joyce first thought of using this word so prominently after reading Samuel Butler's *The Humour of Homer*. One essay in this book, 'Ramblings in Cheapside', has Butler pondering 'how continually we are met by the melting of one existence into another', and finds it everywhere illustrated. 'The doctrine of metempsychosis, or transmigration of souls . . . crops up no matter in what direction we allow our thoughts to wander. And we meet instances of transmigration of body as well as of soul.' A young man Butler saw in the train was unmistakably King Francis I of France. 'His great contemporary Henry VIII keeps a restaurant in Oxford Street. Falstaff drove one of the St. Gotthard diligences for many years, and only retired when the railway was opened. Titian once made me a pair of boots at Vicenza, and not very good ones. At Modena I had my hair cut by a young man whom I perceived to be Raphaelle.' 'Rameses II is a blind woman now, and stands in Holborn, holding a tin cup' (p. 115).

A corroborating indication of Joyce's interest in this book is that another of its chapters, 'The Aunt, the Nieces, and the Dog', contains letters from servant girls, including one as scant of punctuation as Molly Bloom's monologue. In it the writer says 'i feel sure if she tells her young man he will have patient for he is a very kind young man', a phrase that seems linked to Martha Clifford's injunction to Bloom, 'do not deny my request before my patience are exhausted.'

4) There is merriment above (larks) why should there not be high
jinks below stairs?
5) The electric lamps of the gin palace are lit and the boss Roderick
Rex is standing free drinks to all on the 'flure of the house'
6) He is a bit gone in the upper storey, poor jink. Let him lie as he
is (Shem, Ham and Japhet)
7) The birds (doves and ravens) (cf the jinnies is a cooin her hair
and the jinnies is a ravin her hair) he saved escape from his water-
house and leave the zooless patriark alone.

His explanations heap pun upon pun: Noah is a *patriark*, for
example, but even more to the purpose is the way that nine
words, in the process of evoking seven meanings, carry us from
the flood to the rainbow, from China to Ireland, from God to
man, from Browning to Bible, from activities to passivities,
from acceptance to pity. Each pun in effect wreaks havoc with
space and time, and with every form of settled complacency.
Words are fractioned by ineptitude, yet the force that fractions
also draws the world together. Near-misses of sound, sense, and
finally, of form constitute the fabric of creation. Out of malapropisms, spoonerisms, bloomisms, the world is born.

Punning offers then *countersense*, through which disparates are
joined and concordants differentiated. Bloom momentarily
appears to be a dentist of the same name, then is as promptly
re-identified as a canvasser for advertisements. He becomes
Elijah rising in his chariot to heaven, only to have it made
clear that he is as little like Elijah as possible. As he listens to
Simon Dedalus singing the role of Lionel in *Martha*, he is
verbally united with performer and role as 'Siopold'. This
series of doublings and undoublings – for both processes go on
– is one of which heroic and mockheroic are instances. It
pervades Joyce's work as if it were a way in which the artist
could imitate the duplexity of nature.

In *Ulysses* Joyce worked particularly with two kinds of
countersense, which might be called the *undersense* and the
oversense. The *undersense* is a current of sensation, often quite
tangential, which keeps forcing its way to the surface of what
is being thought. So Bloom, on the prowl for lunch, observes

and considers many things; whatever he sees or ponders is flavoured by food. His momentary feeling of depression can find no metaphor except a gustatory one: 'This is the very worst hour of the day . . . Hate this hour. Feel as if I had been eaten and spewed.' Thinking unhappily of Boylan's cold-hearted womanizing, he sees the building he is passing as 'cream curves of stone'. At the cemetery the days of the month take on a mortuary tinge: 'Every Friday buries a Thursday if you come to think of it.' Joyce's method is to present the density of experience by concatenating incongruous sensations and thoughts. He comes close to the quick of the body as it is engaged in its secret transactions with the mind.

The second variety of countersense in Joyce is the *oversense*. Here concepts rather than sensations provide the atmosphere in which quite diverse material becomes enveloped. The first nine chapters of *Ulysses* concede validity to space and time, and the second nine chapters impugn that validity.* The constructive Aristotle is allowed to posit a firm universe of distinct forms and selves, only to have this thrown into confusion by Humean scepticism, and only in the last chapters is stability recoverable, on altered terms. Joyce displays the oversense at work in segregating human behaviour into primarily spatial or primarily temporal activities. Space as oversense requires a geography lesson as time requires a history lesson; when space is in the ascendant, external actions occur, while when time is in the ascendant, the emphasis is on internal processes; space subsumes sculpture as time subsumes music. Such oversenses shape whole chapters of *Ulysses*. In *Finnegans Wake* the same

---

* In *Finnegans Wake* (94) Joyce indicates that the voyage from Alpha to Omega is accomplished first by creating postulates and affirming them, then by questioning them in anticipation of a final affirmation. In this excerpt the nine dots refer to the nine chapters in each half of *Ulysses*:

A . . . . !
? . . . . O

So the first half of the book establishes the connections which the second half throws into doubt before more fully affirming.

pressures determine the characters of Shem and Shaun as they do of the Gracehoper and the Ondt:

> The Ondt was a weltall fellow, raumybult and abelboobied . . .
> He [the Gracehoper] had eaten all the whilepaper, swallowed the lustres, devoured forty flights of styearcases, chewed up all the mensas and seecles . . .   (416)

What is Joyce implying here? I think he is implying first that the system is closed and not open, that the number of human possibilities is limited and that, as we struggle for uniqueness, we discover that we are doing something not for the first time but for the millionth time. But if closed, the system is still fertile. The mind attempts, impartially, to multiply instances of itself in all possible slight variations. Simultaneities are everywhere. 'Think you're escaping and run into your self', says Bloom, as if undoubling were necessarily doubling too.

With this recognition of universal intermingling Joyce attained his final unstated statement about life. Before him as before Whitman stretched democratic vistas, and he could say that he contained multitudes. Yet he did not sentimentalize. What he had discovered was not that all forms were one form – a mystical conclusion – but rather that all forms proceed by incessant doublings and undoublings in which they remain enantiomorphous – that is, resembling each other but not superposable. Hierarchies disappear and the 'aristocracies are supplanted', for all elements are common elements. The pun, verbal emblem of coincidence, agent of democracy and collectivist ideas, makes all the quirky particles of the world stick to each other by hook or crook. Such adhesiveness is unity or the closest to unity that can be envisaged.

Appendix
Joyce's Library in 1920

The following list includes about 600 items which comprise all
or nearly all the library that Joyce left behind him in Trieste
when in June 1920 he moved to Paris. In addition, it includes
about a hundred items, marked with an asterisk, which are not
in the surviving collection but which he can be shown to have
possessed or at least read during the same period. When the
books are stamped 'J.J.', I have so indicated. This was the
stamp which Joyce first used in Zurich and left behind him on
his departure from Trieste in 1920. Regarding place of purchase, see above p. 6.

Books marked with an asterisk belong to the following six
categories:

(At Buffalo) Seven books (by Austen, Butler, Kardec, Plutarch,
Tolstoy, Tucker, Witt) in Joyce's library in Paris. Since they are
stamped 'J.J.', they must date from the period before his move to
Paris.

(Slocum and Cahoon) Books bearing Joyce's signature from his
Dublin days, which are listed in John J. Slocum and Herbert
Cahoon, *A Bibliography of James Joyce, 1882–1941* (New Haven,
Conn., 1953).

(Curran) Books bearing Joyce's signature which are listed in
C. P. Curran, *James Joyce Remembered* (London, 1968), p. 9 n., as
in Curran's possession.

(*Critical Writings*) Books reviewed by Joyce, as indicated in *The
Critical Writings of James Joyce*, ed. Ellsworth Mason and Richard
Ellmann (London and New York, 1959).

(*James Joyce*) Books mentioned in a bookseller's bill (1913–14)
and in an inventory (1920) of part of Joyce's library, published in
Richard Ellmann, *James Joyce* (London and New York, 1959).

(*Letters*) Books which his letters speak of his reading or having
read. See *Letters of James Joyce*, 3 vols. (London and New York,
1957–66).

I have also included one book by John Ruskin on the basis of a photocopy of the title-page with Joyce's dated signature, in the National Library of Ireland.

This list should be supplemented by the list of books which were in the possession of Joyce's family after the Second World War: see Thomas E. Connolly, *The Personal Library of James Joyce* (University of Buffalo Studies, Buffalo, N.Y., 1955). Some of these came into the collection after Joyce's death. For a lively detection from internal evidence of other books that Joyce was reading in the Paris period, see James S. Atherton, *The Books at the Wake* (London and New York, 1960).

Adam of Cobsam, *The Wright's Chaste Wife*, ed. F. J. Furnivall for Early English Text Society (London, 1865)

*Adams, Walter Marsham, *The House of the Hidden Places, A Clue to the Creed of Early Egypt from Egyptian Sources* (London: John Murray, 1895). Inscribed 'Jas A Joyce 1902'.
(Slocum and Cahoon, p. 177)

Aeschylus, *Agamemnon*, trans. into German Hans von Wolzogen (Leipzig: Universal Bibliothek, n.d.). Stamped 'J.J.'

*Ainger, Alfred, *Crabbe* (London: Macmillan, 1903)
(*Critical Writings*, pp. 128–9)

Albert, Charles, *L'Amour libre* (Paris: Stock, 1910). Stamped 'J.J.'

Alfieri, Vittorio, *Vita* [by himself] (Milan: Sonzogno, 1911)

*Allen, Grant, *Paris* (London, ?1897) (*Letters*, II. 25)

—, *The Woman Who Did* (Leipzig: Tauchnitz, 1895)

*Allen, James Lane, *The Mettle of the Pasture* (London: Macmillan, 1903) (*Critical Writings*, pp. 117–18)

Alpha and Omega [pseudonym of Oliver St. John Gogarty], *Blight, The Tragedy of Dublin* (Dublin: Talbot Press, 1917). Stamped 'J.J.'

Alpheo [pseudonym], *The Book of the Land of Ire* (Dublin: Talbot Press, and London: T. Fisher Unwin, 1919). Stamped 'J.J.'

Alvor, Peter, *Das Neue Shakespeare-Evangelium* (Hanover: Adolf Sparholtz Verlag, 1907). (On Shakespeare and Southampton.) Stamped 'J.J.'

Andreyev, Leonid, *Il Riso rosso*, trans. into Italian Cesare Castelli (Milan: Sonzogno, n.d.). Stamped 'J.J.'

—, *The Seven That Were Hanged* (London: A. C. Fifield, 1909)

*Anstie, James, *Colloquies of Common People* (London: Smith, Elder, 1902)   (*Critical Writings*, p. 96)

anthologies of English literature, *see* Barnett, *British Theatre*, E. R. Jones, *Minor Elizabethan Drama*, Morris, Murison, Peacock, Treble, Warren

Apuleius, *Fabula de Psyche et Cupidione* (Rome: Angelo Signorelli, 1918)

Aquinas, Thomas, *Summa Philosophica seu De Veritate Catholicae Fidei* (Paris: P. Lethielleux, n.d.)

—, *Summa Philosophica . . . contra Gentiles* (Paris: P. Lethielleux, 1906)

—, *see also* Rickaby, J.

Arabian Nights (*Le Mille e una notte*), trans. into Italian Armando Dominicis (Florence: Adriana Salani, 1915)

Archer, Patrick, *The Humours of Shanwalla* (Dublin: M. H. Gill, 1906). Stamped 'J.J.'

Aristophanes, *Four Plays* (*Acharnians, Knights, Birds, Frogs*), trans. J. H. Frere (Oxford University Press, 1907). (A previous owner signed his name in January 1909.)

—, *Le Commedie*, vol. II, trans. into Italian Ettore Romagnoli (Milan: Istituto Editoriale Italiano, n.d.). Stamped 'J.J.'

*Aristotle, *Psychology*   (*Letters*, II. 28)

—, *Theory of Poetry and Fine Arts with . . . the Poetics*, trans. with commentary S. H. Butcher (London: Macmillan, 1907). Purchased Trieste.

Arnold, Matthew, *Culture and Anarchy* (London: Thomas Nelson, n.d.). Stamped 'J.J.'

—, *Selected Poems*, 2 vols. (London: Heinemann, 1905). Inscribed by Joyce's fellow Berlitz teacher, Paul Marquardt, 'Berlin, 1905'.

Artzibashef, Michael, *Sanine*, trans. Percy Pinkerton (London: Martin Secker, 1916.) Stamped 'J.J.'

Aurelius Antoninus, Marcus, *The Thoughts*, trans. John Jackson (Oxford University Press, World's Classics, 1906). Stamped 'J.J.'

*Austen, Jane, *Sense and Sensibility* (London: Thomas Nelson, n.d.). Stamped 'J.J.'   (At Buffalo)

Bacon, Francis, *The Wisdom of the Ancients* and *The New Atlantis* (London: Cassell, 1886)
Another copy, published 1900, is stamped 'J.J.'

Bakunin, Michael, *God and the State* (London: Freedom Press, 1910)
                                         (*James Joyce*, p. 794)

Balfour, Andrew, *By Stroke of Sword* (Leipzig: Heinemann and
     Balestier, 1898). (This may not be Joyce's book.)

Balzac, Honoré de, *Béatrix* (Paris: Calmann-Lévy, n.d.)

—, *The Country Doctor*, trans. Ellen Marriage (London: Macmillan,
     1896). Stamped 'J.J.'

—, *L'Enfant maudit* (Paris: Calmann-Lévy, n.d.)

—, *La Femme de trente ans* (Paris: Calmann-Lévy, n.d.)

—, *Histoire des treizes* (Paris: Calmann-Lévy, n.d.)

—, *Louis Lambert* (Paris: Flammarion, n.d.). Purchased Trieste.

—, *Mémoires de deux jeunes mariées* (Paris: Calmann-Lévy, n.d.)

—, *Les Paysans* (Paris: Calmann-Lévy, n.d.)

—, *Petites misères de la vie conjugale* (title page missing)
                                         (*James Joyce*, p. 794)

—, *Physiologie du mariage* (Paris: Calmann-Lévy, n.d.)

—, *La Recherche de l'absolu* (Paris: Calmann-Lévy, n.d.)

—, *Les Rivalités: La Vieille fille* and *Le Cabinet des antiques* (Paris:
     Calmann-Lévy, n.d.)

—, *A Woman of Thirty*, trans. Ellen Marriage (London, 1910).
     Inscribed 'To Nora/Jim/Lady Day 1916'.

Bandello, Matteo, *Le Novelle*, ed. Gioachino Brognoligo, 4 vols.
     (Bari: Gius. Laterza, 1910–11)

Barnett, Annie, and Dale, Lucy, *An Anthology of English Prose (1332
     to 1740)* (London: Longmans Green, 1912). Stamped 'J.J.'
     Purchased Switzerland.

Barrie, J. M., *Peter Pan* (London: Hodder and Stoughton, n.d.).
     Purchased Trieste.

*—, *The Twelve Pound Look*   (*Critical Writings*, p. 250)

Barry, William, *The Papacy and Modern Times* (London: Williams
     and Norgate, n.d.). Signed by Guido Suppan, 1918.

Bartholomew, J. G. *A Literary and Historical Atlas of Europe* (London:
     Dent, and New York: Dutton, Everyman, 1915). Signed by
     Guido Suppan, 1918.

Bassalik-de Vries, J. C. E., *William Blake in His Relation to Dante
     Gabriel Rossetti* (Basel: Brin, 1911). Stamped 'J.J.'

Bazin, René, *The Nun* (New York: Eveleigh Nash, 1908). Stamped
     'J.J.'

Beaumont, Francis, and Fletcher, John, *The Works*, vol. I, including

The Maid's Tragedy, Philaster, A King and No King, The Scornful Lady, The Custom of the Country, ed. Arnold Glover (Cambridge University Press, 1905)

Bédier, Joseph, *Le Roman de Tristan et Iseut* (Paris: Edition d'Art, H. Piazza, n.d.)

—, *The Romance of Tristram and Iseult,* trans. Florence Simmonds (Philadelphia: Lippincott, 1910)

Beethoven, Ludwig van, *Fidelio* (score) (Leipzig: Universal Bibliothek, n.d.). Stamped 'J.J.'

—, *Symphonien Nr. 1–3* (scores) (Leipzig, n.d., but probably about 1 January 1917)

—, *Symphonien Nr. 7–9* (scores) (Leipzig, n.d., but probably about 15 January 1918)

Bellini, Vincenzo, *see* Voss, P.

Belvederian, The (Belvedere College, Dublin), I, no. 1 (Summer 1906)

*Benco, Silvio, *La Fiamma fredda* (Milan, 1904)
(*James Joyce*, p. 794)

*Bérard, Victor, *Les Phéniciens et l'Odyssée,* 2 vols. (Paris, 1902–3)
(*Letters*, I. 401)

Bergson, Henri, *L'Evolution créatrice* (Paris: Félix Alcan, 1914). Purchased Trieste 1913–14.   (*James Joyce*, p. 788)

—, *The Meaning of the War: Life and Matter in Conflict* (London: T. Fisher Unwin, 1915). Stamped 'J.J.'

—, *see also* Solomon, J.

Berkeley, George, *see* Fraser, A. C.

*Berlitz, I. (otherwise unidentified). Purchased 1913–14.
(*James Joyce*, p. 788)

Besant, Annie, *Une Introduction à la Théosophie* (Paris: Publications Théosophiques, 1907). Stamped 'J.J.'

—, *The Path of Discipleship* (London: Theosophical Publishing Society, 1904). Stamped 'J.J.' Acquired on or after 24 March 1906.

Bible (King James version) (London, 1825)

—, see *Sacra Bibbia, La*

Biblia Sacra (Vulgate), ed. Valentinus Loch, 2 vols. [1902]. Stamped 'J.J.'

Bizet, Georges, *see* Voss, P.

Björnson, Björnstjerne, *The Fisher Lass* (London: Heinemann, 1908). Stamped 'J.J.'

Blake, William, *Poems of*, ed. W. B. Yeats (London: Routledge, Muses' Library [June 1905])

—, *The Poems*, with prefatory note by Joseph Skipsey (London: Walter Scott, n.d.). Purchased Trieste.

—, *The Poetical Works of*, ed. William Michael Rossetti (London: George Bell, 1911)

Blakeney, E. H., *see Smaller Classical Dictionary*, *A*

Bleibtreu, Carl, *Das Byron-Geheimnis* (Munich and Leipzig: George Müller, 1912). Stamped 'J.J.'

Bodkin, Richard, *Logic for All* (Dublin: Browne and Nolan, 1910). Stamped 'J.J.'

Boehme, Jacob, *The Signature of All Things* (London: Dent, Everyman, [1912]). *(James Joyce*, p. 794)

Boileau, Nicolas, *Le Lutrin* (Paris: Henri Gautier, n.d.) (Bibliothèque Populaire Nouvelle, no. 361)

*Boine, Giovanni, *Il Peccato* *(James Joyce*, p. 794)

Bonn, M. J., *Irland und die Irische Frage* (Munich and Leipzig: Verlag Duncker and Humblot, 1918). Stamped 'J.J'

Bormann, Edwin, *Francis Bacon's Cryptic Rhymes* (London: Siegle, Hill, 1906)

Bossuet, Jacques-Bénigne, *Sermons Choisis* (Paris: Librairie Firmin Dodot Frères, 1860)

Bourget, Paul, *Sensations d'Italie* (Paris: Alphonse Lemerre, 1891)

Boyle, John F., *The Irish Rebellion of 1916* (London: Constable, 1916). Stamped 'J.J.'

Boyle, William, *The Building Fund* (Dublin: M. H. Gill, 1916). Stamped 'J.J.'

—, *Family Failing* (Dublin: M. H. Gill, 1912). Stamped 'J.J.'

—, *The Mineral Workers* (Dublin: M. H. Gill, 1916). Stamped 'J.J.'

*Bracciforti, Ferdinando, *Chiave dei temi sceneggiati*
(James Joyce, p. 794)

*—, *Grammatica della lingua inglese* *(James Joyce*, p. 794)

Brachet, Auguste, *The Public School Elementary French Grammar*, (2 parts) adapted by P. H. E. Brette and Gustave Masson, revised by E. Janau (London and Paris: Hachette, 1891). Both (John) Stanislaus Joyce and James A. Joyce have signed their names in the book.

Brandes, George, *William Shakespeare, A Critical Study* (London: Heinemann, 1911)

Brillat-Savarin, *Physiologie du goût ou Méditations de gastronomie transcendante* (Paris: Garnier Frères, n.d.). Stamped 'J.J.'

Britisches gegen Deutsches Imperium (Anon.), with a Foreword by Roger Casement (Berlin: Verlag Gebrüder Paetel, 1915). Stamped 'J.J.'

British Theatre comprising Tragedies, Comedies, Operas and Farces (Leipzig: Frederick Fleischer, 1828)

Brontë, Charlotte, *Jane Eyre* (London: Faudel, Phillips, n.d.). Stamped 'J.J.' Apparently used for teaching purposes in 1912.

Brontë family, *see* Leyland, F. A.

Browning, Robert, *Selections from the Poetical Works* (London: Smith, Elder, 1891)

Bruno, Giordano, *Degli Eroici furori*, 2 vols. (Milan: Sonzogno, 1906). Purchased Trieste.

Bulwer-Lytton, Edward, *The Last Days of Pompeii* (Leipzig: Tauchnitz, 1879)

Bunyan, John, *Pilgrim's Progress* (London: Religious Tract Society, n.d.)

Burke, Thomas, *Limehouse Nights* (London: Grant Richards, 1917). Stamped 'J.J.'

*Burnet, John, *Aristotle on Education* (Cambridge University Press, 1903)   (*Critical Writings*, pp. 109–10)

Burns, Robert, *The Poetical Works* (Oxford University Press, World's Classics, 1919)

—, *The Poetical Works of* (Halifax: Milner and Sowerby, 1855)

[Burton, Richard], *The Anatomy of Melancholy* (London: B. Blake, 1836). Stamped 'J.J.'

Busoni, Ferruccio, *Entwurf einer neuen Ästhetik der Tonkunst* (Leipzig: Insel-verlag, ?1919). Stamped 'J.J.'

Butler, O'Brien, *Seven Original Irish Melodies* (Belfast: Pigott, 1903). Inscribed by Butler to Joyce, 29 April 1910.

*Butler, Samuel, *The Authoress of the Odyssey* (London: A. C. Fifield, [1897]). Stamped 'J.J.'   (At Buffalo)

—, *Erewhon* (London: A. C. Fifield, 1917). Stamped 'J.J.'

—, *The Humour of Homer* (London: A. C. Fifield, 1913). Stamped 'J.J.'

—, *Shakespeare's Sonnets* (London: A. C. Fifield, [1899]). Stamped 'J.J.' Purchased after 29 September 1917.

Butler, Samuel, *The Way of all Flesh* (London: A. C. Fifield, 1911). Stamped 'J.J.'

Byington, S. T., *see* Eltzbacher, P.

Byron, Lord, *Poems* (London: Routledge, n.d.). Stamped 'J.J.'

—, *see also* Jeaffreson, J. C.

Byron, May, *A Day with Richard Wagner* (London: Hodder and Stoughton, [1911])

—, *see also* Clare, M.

*Cameron, Mrs. Lovett, *A Difficult Matter* (London: John Long, 1898)   (*Letters*, II. 82)

Campanella, Tommaso, *Apologia di Galileo e Dialogo politico contro Luterani* etc. (Lanciano: Carabba Editore, 1911)

—, *La Città del sole* (Milan: Sonzogno, n.d.). Stamped 'J.J.' (Another edition: Lanciano: Carabba Editore, n.d.)

*Campbell, Joseph, *Judgment* (Dublin: Maunsel, 1912)
                                    (*James Joyce*, p. 794)

*Canning, A. S. *Shakespeare Studied in Eight Plays* (London: T. Fisher Unwin, 1903)   (*Critical Writings*, pp. 137–8)

Caprin, Giulio, *Trieste e l'italia* (Milan: Rava, 1915). Stamped 'J.J.'

Carlyle, Thomas, *The French Revolution* (London: Chapman and Hall, n.d.). Signed Guido Suppan, 1920.

—, *Past and Present* (Oxford University Press, World's Classics, 1909)

*Caryl, Valentine [pseudonym], *A Ne'er-Do-Weel* (London: T. Fisher Unwin, 1903)   (*Critical Writings*, pp. 111–12)

Casement, Roger, *see Britisches gegen Deutsches Imperium*

Cattaneo, Carlo, *Saggi di filosofia civile* and *Ricerche economiche sulle interdizioni imposta dalla legge civile agli Israelitici* (Milan: Sonzogno, 1911)

Cervantes, Michele, *Il Dialogo dei cani* (Milan: Sonzogno, n.d.). Stamped 'J.J.' Purchased Zurich.

Chateaubriand, François-René de, *Atala* (Paris: Flammarion, n.d., title page missing). Stamped 'J.J.'

Chaucer, Geoffrey, *The Canterbury Tales* (digest with excerpts) (London, n.d.). Stamped 'J.J.'

—, *The Complete Works*, ed. W. W. Skeat (Oxford University Press, 1915). Stamped 'J.J.'

*Chennevière, Daniel, *Claude Debussy*. Purchased Trieste, 1913–14.
                                    (*James Joyce*, p. 788)

Cicero, Marcus Tullius, *Tusculanarum Disputationum*, ed. C. F. W. Muller (Leipzig: Teubner, 1888)

Clare, Maurice [pseudonym of May Byron], *A Day with William Shakespeare* (London: Hodder and Stoughton, [1913]). Stamped 'J.J.'

Coleridge, Samuel Taylor, *Lectures and Notes on Shakespeare* (London: George Bell, 1907)

*Colette, *Claudine à l'école*   (*James Joyce*, p. 795)

Collier, William Francis, *History of Ireland* [for schools] (London: Marcus Ward, n.d.). Stamped 'J.J.'

Collins, W. Lucas, *Homer: The Iliad* (a study) (Edinburgh and London: Blackwood, 1887)

*Collodi, Carlo, *Pinocchio*. Purchased Trieste, 1913–14.
                                                   (*James Joyce*, p. 788)

Colum, Padraic, *The Fiddler's House* (Dublin: Maunsel, 1905)

—, *The Land* (Dublin: Maunsel, 1905)

—, *Studies* (Dublin: Maunsel, 1907). Includes 'The Miracle of the Corn', 'Eilis: A Woman's Story', 'The Flute Player's Story'.

—, *Thomas Muskerry* (Dublin: Maunsel, 1910)

Conrad, Joseph, *Chance*, 2 vols. (Leipzig: Tauchnitz, 1914)

—, *The Nigger of the 'Narcissus'* (London: Heinemann, 1916). Stamped 'J.J.'

—, *The Secret Agent* (Leipzig: Tauchnitz, 1907)

—, *A Set of Six* (Leipzig: Tauchnitz, 1908)   (*Letters*, II. 283)

—, *Tales of Unrest* (Leipzig: Tauchnitz, 1898)

—, *Within the Tides* (Paris: Louis Conard, 1915). Stamped 'J.J.'

Constant, Benjamin, *Adolphe* (Paris, London, New York: Dent, n.d.) (in French). Stamped 'J.J.'

*Corelli, Marie, *The Sorrows of Satan* (London: Methuen, 1895)
                                                       (*Letters*, II. 82)

*—, *Ziska, The Problem of a Wicked Soul* (London: Simpkin, Marshall, 1897)   (*Letters*, II. 83)

Cousins, Herbert H., *The Chemistry of the Garden* (London: Macmillan, 1903). Stamped 'J.J.'

Dana (Dublin)   (*James Joyce*, p. 795)

*D'Annunzio, Gabriele, *The Child of Pleasure*, trans. Georgina Harding, with introduction and verse translation by Arthur Symons (London: Heinemann, 1898). Inscribed 'Jas A. Joyce Mullingar July. 5. 1900'.   (Slocum and Cahoon, p. 176)

*D'Annunzio, Gabriele, *La Figlia de Iorio* (Milan, 1904)
(*Letters*, II. 76)

*—, *La Gioconda* (Milan, 1900). Signed and dated 'May 1900' by Joyce. (Curran, p. 9)

—, *Giovanni episcopo* (Florence: Editore Quattrini, 1917). Stamped 'J.J.'

*—, *La Gloria* (Milan, 1899). Signed and dated 'September 1900' by Joyce. (Curran, p. 9)

*—, *Sogno d'un tramonto d'autumno* (Milan, 1899). Signed and dated 'September 1900' by Joyce. (Curran, p. 9)

Dante Alighieri, *La Divina commedia*, ed. Eugenio Camerini (Milan: Sonzogno, n.d.). Stamped 'J.J.'

—, *La Vita nuova* (Turin: Edizioni STEN, 1911), with illustrations by D. G. Rossetti. Signed and dated 16 October 1912 by previous owner.

Daudet, Alphonse, *Aventures prodigieuses de Tartarin de Tarascon*, ed. O. H. Brandt (Vienna: Tempsky, and Leipzig: Freytag, 1911)

Davitt, Michael, *The Fall of Feudalism in Ireland* (London and New York: Harper and Bros., 1904). Stamped 'J.J.'

De Amicis, Edmondo, *Ricordi di Parigi* (Milan: Fratelli Treves, 1908). Stamped 'J.J.'

—, *La Vita militare* (Naples: Salvatore Romano, 1912)

Debussy, Claude, *see* Chennevière, D.

Defoe, Daniel, *Works*, I, including *Captain Singleton* and *Colonel Jack* (London: George Bell, 1908). Signed by Stanislaus Joyce.

—, *Works*, II, including *Memoirs of Captain Carleton*, *Dickory Cronke*, *Everybody's Business*, *Memoirs of a Cavalier* (London: George Bell, 1906)

—, *Works*, IV, including *Roxana, or The Fortunate Mistress* and *Mrs. Christian Davies* (London: George Bell, 1910). Signed by Stanislaus Joyce.

De Morgan, William, *Joseph Vance*, 2 vols. (Leipzig: Tauchnitz, 1911) (*Letters*, I. 101)

Dickens, Charles, *Barnaby Rudge* (London: Thomas Nelson, [1912]). Purchased Trieste.

—, *Bleak House* (London: Bradbury and Evans, 1853)

—, *David Copperfield* (London: Thomas Nelson, [1912]). Purchased Trieste.

—, *Nicholas Nickleby*, 2 vols. (London: Chapman & Hall, [1912])

—, *Oliver Twist* (London: Thomas Nelson, [1912]). Same edition as *David Copperfield*.

*Disraeli, Benjamin, *Lothair* (London, 1870) (*Letters*, II. 86)

d'Ivray, Jehan, *Memoires de l'eunuque Bechir-Aga* (Paris: Albin Michel, n.d.). Stamped 'J.J.' Purchased Switzerland.

Dobson, Austin, *Eighteenth Century Studies* (London: Dent, n.d.)

*Dodge, Janet, ed., *Twelve Elizabethan Songs* (London, 1902)
(*Letters*, II. 35)

Dostoevsky, Fyodor, *Crime and Punishment* (London: Heinemann, 1916). Stamped 'J.J.'

—, *The Idiot* (London: Heinemann, 1913). Purchased Trieste, 1913–14. (*James Joyce*, p. 788)

Dovizi, Bernardo, *Calandra* (Rome: Oreste Garroni, 1910)

*Doyle, A. Conan, *The Tragedy of the Korosko, etc.* (London: Smith, Elder, 1898) (*Letters*, II. 83)

Dujardin, Edouard, *L'Initiation au peché et à l'amour* (Paris: Mercure de France, 1912). Stamped 'J.J.'

*—, *Les Lauriers sont coupés* (*Letters*, II. 409)

—, *La Source du fleuve chrétien* (Paris: Mercure de France, 1906). Stamped 'J.J.'

Early English Text Society, *see* Adam of Cobsam

Eglinton, John [pseudonym of W. K. Magee], *Anglo-Irish Essays* (Dublin: Talbot Press, and London: T. Fisher Unwin, 1917). Stamped 'J.J.'

—, *Bards and Saints* (Dublin: Maunsel, Tower Press Booklet No. 5, 1906) (*James Joyce*, p. 794)

Egoist, The, issue of 16 February 1914. Purchased Trieste, 1914.
(*James Joyce*, p. 788)

Eliot, George, *The Mill on the Floss* (Leipzig: Tauchnitz, 1886)
(*James Joyce*, p. 794)
Another copy (Dent, Everyman, 1914). Stamped 'J.J.'

—, *Romola* (London: Smith, Elder, 1875)

Ellis, Havelock, *The New Spirit* (London etc.: Walter Scott, n.d., Preface dated 1892)

Eltzbacher, Paul, *Anarchism*, trans. S. T. Byington (New York: Benjamin R. Tucker, and London: A. C. Fifield, 1908). Purchased Trieste, 1913–14. (*James Joyce*, p. 788)

Elze, Karl, *William Shakespeare* (London: George Bell, 1901)

Epictetus, *The Teachings*, trans. T. W. Rolleston (London and Felling-on-Tyne: Walter Scott, n.d.)

Ervine, St. John G., *Changing Winds* (Dublin: Maunsel, 1917). Stamped 'J.J.'

*—, *Mixed Marriage* (Dublin: Maunsel, 1911)

(*James Joyce*, p. 794)

Euclid, *see* Hall, H. S. and Stevens, F. H.

Euripides, *Le Baccanti*, trans. into Italian Ettore Romagnoli (Florence: A. Quattrini, 1912)

Everyman (play)   (*Letters*, II. 35)

Every Man's Own Lawyer (London: Crosby Lockwood, 1919). Stamped 'J.J.'

Fabian Tracts, nos. 1–173 (bound together) (London: Fabian Society, 1884–1913)

Farrar, F. W., *The Life and Work of St. Paul*, 2 vols. (London: Cassell, Petter, Galpin, n.d., but Preface dated 1879)

Fénelon, Salignac de la Mothe, *Les Aventures de Télémaque* (Paris: Flammarion, n.d.)

*Ferrero, Guglielmo, *L'Europa giovane*

(*James Joyce*, p. 794; *Letters*, II. 133, 190)

Fielding, Henry, *Amelia* (London: Routledge, n.d.)

—, *Joseph Andrews*, 2 vols. (Dresden, 1783)

*Fielding-Hall, H., *The Soul of a People* (London: Richard Bentley, 1898)   (*Critical Writings*, pp. 93–5)

First Catechism (London and Madras: Christian Literature Society for India, 1896). Stamped 'J.J.'

FitzGerald, Edward, *Rubaiyat of Omar Khayyam* (Leipzig: Tauchnitz, 1910)

Fitzpatrick, William J., *Curious Family History; or, Ireland Before the Union* (Dublin: W. B. Kelly, 1870). Stamped 'J.J.'

—, '*The Sham Squire*,' *and The Informers of 1798* (Dublin: M. H. Gill, n.d., Preface dated 1865). Stamped 'J.J.'

Flaubert, Gustave, *Madame Bovary*, trans. Henry Blanchamp (London: Greening, n.d.). Stamped 'J.J.'

—, *Premières Oeuvres*, 2 vols. (Paris: Bibliothèque Charpentier, 1914). Purchased Trieste, 1914.   (*James Joyce*, p. 788)

—, *Salammbô* (Paris: Bibliothèque Charpentier, 1914). Stamped 'J.J.'

*—, *La Tentation de Saint Antoine*. Purchased Trieste, 1913–14.
(*James Joyce*, p. 788)

*Fogazzaro, Antonio, *Piccolo mondo antico* (Milan: Baldini, Castoldie, 1900). Signed 'JAJ'. (Slocum and Cahoon, p. 177)

*—, *Piccolo Mondo moderno* (Milan: Hoepli, 1901). Signed 'Jas A Joyce. 1902'. (Slocum and Cahoon, p. 178)

Foscolo, Ugo, *Ultime lettere di Jacopo Ortis* (Sesto S. Giovanni: Casa Editrice Madello, 1912)

*France, Anatole, *L'Affaire Crainquebille* (*Letters*, II. 212)

*—, *Monsieur Bergeret à Paris* (*Letters*, II. 85)

Francis, J. O., *Change, A Glamorgan Play in Four Acts* (Cardiff: Educational Publishing Co., 1910) (2 copies, both stamped 'J.J.')

Fraser, Alexander Campbell, *Berkeley* (Edinburgh: Blackwood, 1912). Stamped 'J.J.' Purchased Zurich.

Freeman, Edward A., *General Sketch of European History* (London: Macmillan, 1895). Stamped 'J.J.'

Freud, Sigmund, *Eine Kindheitserinnerung des Leonardo da Vinci* (Leipzig and Vienna, 1910). Purchased in Trieste (price Kroner 3.10).

—, *Zur Psychopathologie des Alltaglebens* (Berlin, 1917). Stamped 'J.J.' Purchased Zurich.

Funk, S., *Die Entstehung des Talmuds* (Leipzig: G. J. Göscher, 1910)

Galopin, Augustin, *Le Parfum de la femme* (Paris: E. Dentu, 1889). Stamped 'J.J.' Purchased Zurich.

Galsworthy, John, *Justice and Other Plays* (Leipzig: Tauchnitz, 1912)

Garnier, P., *Onanisme seul et à deux sous toutes ses formes et leurs conséquences* (Paris: Librairie Garnier Frères, n.d.). Stamped 'J.J.' Purchased Switzerland.

Gaskell, Mrs., *Ruth* (London: Chapman and Hall, 1867). Stamped 'J.J.'

Gaultier, Bon [pseudonym of Sir Theodore Martin], *The Book of Ballads* (Edinburgh and London: Blackwood, 1874)

Gide, André, *L'Immoraliste* (Paris: Mercure de France, 1914)

Gilbert, W. S., *Original Plays* (London: Chatto and Windus, 1911)

*Gissing, George, *The Crown of Life* (London: Methuen, 1899)
(*Letters*, II. 189)

*—, *Demos* (London: Smith, Elder, 1886) (*Letters*, II. 186)

Glebe, The, I, no. 5 (February 1914), *Des Imagistes* issue
(*Letters,* II. 328)

Gluck, C. W., *Orpheus and Eurydice* (Leipzig: Universal Bibliothek, n.d.). Stamped 'J.J.'

*Glyn, Elinor, *Visits of Elizabeth* (London: Duckworth, 1900)
(*Letters,* II. 83)

Godwin, William, *Caleb Williams* (London: Routledge, 1903). Stamped 'J.J.'

Goethe, Johann Wolfgang von, *Novels and Tales* (*Elective Affinities, The Sorrows of Werther, Certain Emigrants, The Good Women,* and *A Tale*), trans. J. A. Froude and R. D. Boylan (London: George Bell, 1911)

Gogarty, Oliver St. John, *see* Alpha and Omega

Gogol, Nicolai, *Tarass Bulba,* trans. into Italian anonymously (Milan: Editrice Lombarda, 1877)

Goldoni, Carlo, *La Donna sola* (Rome: Edoardo Perino, 1893)

Goldsmith, Oliver, *The Select Works of* (Leipzig: Tauchnitz, 1842)

*—, *The Vicar of Wakefield* (*Letters,* II. 99)

—, *The Works* (London: John Dicks, n.d.). Stamped 'J.J.'

Golther, Wolfgang, *Richard Wagner as Poet,* trans. Jessie Haynes (London: Heinemann, 1905)

Gorky, Maxim, *L'Albergo dei poveri,* trans. into Italian E. W. Foulques (Naples, 1905)

—, *Il Burlone, L'Angoscia,* trans. into Italian E. W. Foulques (Naples: Salvatore Romano, 1906)

—, *I Fasti della rivoluzione russa* (Naples, n.d.)

—, *Le Passeggiate del diavolo,* trans. into Italian E. W. Foulques (Naples, 1907)

*Graves, Arnold, *Clytaemnestra: A Tragedy* (London: Longmans, 1903)   (*Critical Writings,* pp. 126–7)

Greene, E. A., *Saints and Their Symbols* (London: Whitaker, 1913). Stamped 'J.J.' Purchased Zurich.

Gregg, J. A. F., ed., *The Wisdom of Solomon* (part of the Cambridge Bible) (Cambridge University Press, 1909). Stamped 'J.J.'

Gregory, Augusta, Lady, *The Kiltartan Wonder Book* (Dublin: Maunsel, [1910])

—, *Poets and Dreamers* (Dublin: Hodges Figgis, 1903)
(*Critical Writings,* pp. 102–5)

—, *Spreading the News, The Rising of the Moon*; Douglas Hyde and

Lady Gregory, *The Poor-House* (Dublin: Maunsel, 1907). Purchased Trieste.

—, *The White Cockade* (Dublin: Maunsel, 1905)

(*James Joyce*, p. 795)

Griffith, Arthur, *The Finance of the Home Rule Bill* (Dublin: National Council, 1912)

—, *The Home Rule Examined* (Dublin: National Council, 1912)

*Guide to Troubadours (*James Joyce*, p. 794)

[Guillermet, Fanny], *Autour de la Grève générale* (Neuchâtel: Attinger Frères, Nov. 1918). Inscribed by her to Joyce 3 January 1919.

—, *Et Nous?* (Neuchâtel: Attinger Frères, Feb. 1919). Inscribed by her to Joyce 2 March 1919.

—, *Le Frein* (Neuchâtel: Attinger Frères, Dec. 1918). Inscribed by her to Joyce 2 March 1919.

*Gwynn, Stephen, *To-day and To-morrow in Ireland* (Dublin: Hodges Figgis, 1903)   (*Critical Writings*, pp. 90–2)

Haig, Alexander, *Uric Acid: An Epitome of the Subject* (London: J. and A. Churchill, 1904). Stamped 'J.J.' Purchased Switzerland.

Haggard, H. Rider, *She* (London: Readers Library, n.d.)

Hall, H. S., and Stevens, F. H., *A Text-Book of Euclid's Elements* (London: Macmillan, 1900). Stamped 'J.J.'

*Hamsun, Knut, *Aftenrøde*   (*James Joyce*, p. 794)

*—, *Livets spil*   (*James Joyce*, p. 794)

*—, *Ved rigets port*   (*James Joyce*, p. 794)

*Hardy, Thomas, *Life's Little Ironies* (London: McIlvaine, 1894)

(*Letters*, II. 198–9)

—, *Tess of the D'Urbervilles*, 2 vols. (Leipzig: Tauchnitz, 1892)

*Harte, Bret, *Gabriel Conroy* (Boston and New York, 1903)

(*Letters*, II. 166)

—, *Tales of the West* (London: T. Nelson, n.d.). Stamped 'J.J.'

*Hauptmann, Gerhart, *The Coming of Peace*, trans. Janet Achurch and C. E. Wheeler (London: Duckworth, 1900). Signed and dated 'February 1900' by Joyce.   (Curran, p. 9)

*—, *Elga*   (*Letters*, II. 85)

*—, *Hannele, A Dream Poem*, trans. William Archer (London: Heinemann, 1894). Signed and dated 'August 1900' by Joyce.

(Curran, p. 9)

*—, *Michael Kramer* (Translated by Joyce.)   (*Letters*, II. 58)

Hauptmann, Gerhart, *Die Ratten* (Berlin: G. Fischer, 1911). Signed by A. Ralli. Obtained Trieste.

—, *Rosa Bernd*, trans. into Italian Cesare Castelli (Rome: Enrico Voghera, 1906) *(Letters*, II. 152, 173)

*—, *Vor Sonnenaufgang* (Translated by Joyce.) *(Letters*, II. 58)

*—, *The Weavers* *(Letters*, II. 173)

Hazlitt, William, *Characters of Shakespeare's Plays*, ed. W. C. Hazlitt (London: George Bell, 1908)

—, *Lectures on the Literature of the Age of Elizabeth Chiefly Dramatic*, ed. W. C. Hazlitt (London: George Bell, 1909)

*Heijermans, Hermann, *Ahasver* *(Letters*, II. 85)

Henke, Oskar, *Die Gedichte Homers*, Erster Teil: *Die Odyssee* (commentary on words and phrases) (Leipzig and Berlin: B. G. Teubner, 1906). Stamped 'J.J.' Purchased Zurich.

Herzl, Theodor, *Der Judenstaat* (Berlin: Jüdische Verlag, 1918). Stamped 'J.J.' Purchased Zurich.

High History of the Holy Graal, The, trans. Sebastian Evans (London: Everyman, n.d.). *See also* Perceval, le Gallois.

History of Excess *(James Joyce*, p. 794)

*Hodgson, William Ballantyne, *Errors in the Use of English* (Edinburgh, 1881) *(James Joyce*, p. 794)

*Holdsworth, William, *The Law of Wills* *(James Joyce*, p. 794)

Holmes, Oliver Wendell, *The Autocrat of the Breakfast Table* (Boston and New York: Houghton Mifflin, 1892)

—, *Ralph Waldo Emerson* (London: Kegan Paul, Trench, 1885)

Homer, *Iliad*, trans. Edward Earl of Derby (London: Dent, Everyman, 1914). Stamped 'J.J.'

—, *Il Libro XIV dell'Odissea*, ed. Salvatore Rossi (Leghorn: R. Giusti, 1915)

—, *L'Odissea*, Book I (with interlinear translation in Italian) (Rome and Milan: Albrighi, Segati, 1905)

—, *Odyssey*, trans. William Cowper (London, Dent, Everyman, 1913). Stamped 'J.J.'

—, *see also* Collins, W. L. *and* Henke, O.

*Horton, William Thomas, *A Book of Images*, drawn by Horton and introduced by W. B. Yeats (London: Unicorn Press, 1898). Inscribed 'Jas A Joyce. 1901'. (Slocum and Cahoon, p. 177)

Hueffer, Francis, *The Troubadours* (London: Chatto and Windus, 1878). Acquired Trieste. *(James Joyce*, p. 795)

Hume, David, *Essays*: I. *An Inquiry Concerning Human Understanding*; II. *An Inquiry Concerning the Principles of Morals* (London: Watts, 1906). Purchased Trieste.

—, *The History of England*, 8 vols. (London: Cadell and Davies, 1818)

Humperdinck, Engelbert, *Hänsel and Gretel* (libretto) (Elberfeld: Lucas, n.d.). Stamped 'J.J.'

Humphreys, E. M. J., *see* Rita

Huxley, Thomas Henry, *Twelve Lectures and Essays* (London: Watts, 1908)

*Huysmans, Joris-Karl, *A Rebours* (Paris, 1884)   (*Letters*, II. 150)

*—, *Là-Bas* (Paris: Stock, 1901). Inscribed 'Jas A Joyce 1901'.
(Slocum and Cahoon, p. 177)

Hyde, Douglas, *Love Songs of Connacht* (London: T. Fisher Unwin, and Dublin: M. H. Gill, 1905). Stamped 'J.J.'

—, *see* Gregory, A.

Ibsen, Henrik, *Baumeister Solness*, trans. into German Sigurd Ibsen (Leipzig: Universal Bibliothek, n.d.). Stamped 'J.J.'

*—, *Bygmester Solness* (Copenhagen: Gyldendalske Boghandels Forlag, 1892). Signed and dated 'Jas. Joyce, April 1901'.
(At Buffalo. Slocum and Cahoon, p. 177; *Letters*, II. 183)

*—, *Catilina* (Paris, ?1903)   (*Critical Writings*, pp. 98–101)

—, *Collected Works*, I: *Lady Inger of Östråt*, *The Feast at Solhoug* [*Letters*, II. 83], *Love's Comedy*, trans. by various hands (London: Heinemann, 1910); II: *The Vikings at Helgeland*, *The Pretenders*, trans. William Archer (London: Heinemann, 1910); III: *Brand*, trans. V. H. Herford (London: Heinemann, 1908); IV: *Peer Gynt*, trans. William and Charles Archer (London: Heinemann, 1912); VII: *A Doll's House*, *Ghosts*, trans. William Archer (London: Heinemann, 1912). Vols. IV and VII were purchased Trieste, and probably I, II, and III as well.
(*James Joyce*, p. 788)

—, *Hedda Gabler*, trans. Edmund Gosse (London: Heinemann and Balestier, 1891)

—, *John Gabriel Borkman*, trans. into German (Berlin: S. Fischer, 1910). Stamped 'J.J.'   (*Letters*, I. 51–2)

*—, *Nar vi Döde Vågner* (Copenhagen and London: Heinemann, 1899). Inscribed 'Jas. Joyce 1901'.
(Slocum and Cahoon, p. 177; *Critical Writings*, pp. 47–67)

Ibsen, Henrik, *Ein Volksfeind*, trans. into German by Wilhelm Lange (Leipzig: Universal Bibliothek, n.d.). Stamped 'J.J.'

*—, *The Wild Duck*. Acquired by 1904. (Curran, p. 9)

—, *see also* Levertin, O.

Imagistes, Des, see *Glebe, The*

Irish Review (Dublin: Cuala Press, 1912). Contains James Stephens, 'How the Husband of the Thin Woman Lost His Brother', pp. 296–303.

*Jacobsen, J. P., *Mogens* (1882) (*Letters*, II. 83)

—, *Siren Voices* [*Niels Lyhne*], trans. E. F. L. Robertson (London: Heinemann, 1896). Stamped 'J.J.' (*Letters*, II. 83)

James, G. P. R., *Forest Days* (Paris: Galignani, 1843)

*James, Henry, *Confidence* (London: Chatto and Windus, 1879)
(*Letters*, II. 85)

*—, *French Poets and Novelists* (London: Macmillan, 1878)
(*Letters*, II. 76)

*—, *The Madonna of the Future* (*Letters*, II. 71)

Jameson, Mrs., *Shakespeare's Heroines* (London: Dent, 1910)

Jammes, Francis, *Le Roman du lièvre* (Paris: Mercure de France, 1914)

Jeaffreson, John Cordy, *The Real Lord Byron*, 3 vols. in 1 (Leipzig: Tauchnitz, 1883)

Jefferies, Richard, *see* Thomas, E.

Jerome, Jerome K., *Novel Notes* (London: Leadenhall Press, 1893). Inscription says 'Stolen from Stanislaus Joyce by the present owner'.

*Jerrold, Walter, *George Meredith* (London: Greening, 1902)
(*Critical Writings*, pp. 88–9)

Johnson, Samuel, *The Lives of the English Poets*, 2 vols. in 1 (Leipzig: Tauchnitz, 1858)

—, *The Rambler*, 3 vols. (London, 1810)

*—, *Rasselas* (*James Joyce*, p. 795)

Jones, Edgar R., ed., *Selected English Speeches from Burke to Gladstone* (Oxford University Press, World's Classics, 1913). Stamped 'J.J.'

Jones, Ernest, *Das Problema des Hamlet und des Ödipus-Komplex*, trans. into German Paul Tausig (Leipzig and Vienna, 1911). Purchased Trieste.

Joyce, James, *Chamber Music* (London: Elkin Mathews, 1907). Stamped 'J.J.'

—, *Verbannte*, trans. Hannah von Mettal (Zurich: Rascher, 1919). Inscribed to Stanislaus Joyce, 7 August 1919. Another copy published Berlin by Oesterheld.

Jung, C. G., *Die Bedeutung des Vaters dur das Schicksal des Einzelnen* (Leipzig and Vienna, 1909). Purchased Trieste.

Junius, 2 vols. (London: Vernor and Hood, 1805)

*Kardec, Allan, *La Genèse: Les Miracles et les prédictions selon le spiritisme* (Paris: Librairie des Sciences Psychologiques, 1883). Stamped 'J.J.'   (At Buffalo)

Kavanagh, M., *Shemus Dhu, The Black Peddler of Galway* (Dublin: Duffy, 1881). Stamped 'J.J.'

Keats, John, *Poems* (London: Methuen, 1903)

Keller, Gottfried, *Der Grüne Heinrich*, 3 vols. (Zurich: Rascher, 1918). Stamped 'J.J.'

—, *Romeo und Julia auf dem Dorfe* (Zurich: Verein fur Verbreitung guter Schriften, February 1919). Stamped 'J.J.'

Kelly, H. P., *Irish Bulls and Puns* (London: Skeffington, n.d.). Stamped 'J.J.'

Kempis, Thomas à, *The Imitation of Christ*, trans. R. Challoner (Dublin: Gill, n.d.). Signed 'A.M.D.G. Jas. A. Joyce October 26th 1897'.

*Kempster, Aquila, *The Adventures of Prince Aga Mirza* (London: T. Fisher Unwin, 1903)   (*Critical Writings*, p. 116)

Kerr, S. Parnell, *What the Irish Regiments Have Done* (London: T. Fisher Unwin, 1916). Stamped 'J.J.'

Kettle, Thomas M., *Home Rule Finance: An Experiment in Justice* (Dublin: Maunsel, 1911)   (*Letters*, II. 287)

—, *Irish Orators and Oratory* (Dublin: Talbot Press, [1908?]). Stamped 'J.J.'

—, *The Ways of War*, with a Memoir by Mary S. Kettle (London: Constable, 1917). Stamped 'J.J.'

Kipling, Rudyard, *A Diversity of Creatures* (Paris: Louis Conard, 1917). Stamped 'J.J.'

—, *Kim* (Leipzig: Tauchnitz, 1901)

—, *The Light that Failed* (Leipzig: Heinemann and Balestier, 1892)

*—, *Plain Tales from the Hills* (London, 1888)   (*Letters*, II. 205)

—, *Stalky & Co.* (Leipzig: Tauchnitz, 1899). Acquired Trieste, probably in 1912.

Kipling, Rudyard, *The Story of the Gadsbys* and *Under the Deodars* (Leipzig: Heinemann and Balestier, 1891). Signed by Guido Suppan, 'June 1914'.

Kock, Paul de, *Le Cocu* (Gand: Vandenhaeghe Maya, 1839). Purchased Trieste.   (*James Joyce*, p. 794)

Koemmenich, Louis, 'O Cool Is the Valley Now' (music) (New York: Fischer, 1919)

Kohl, J. G., *Ireland, Scotland and England* (London: Chapman and Hall, 1844). Travel book.

Kropotkin, Peter, *The Commune of Paris* (London: 'Freedom' Office, 1909)

—, *La Conquista del pane*, 3rd ed. (Milan: n.d.). Stamped 'J.J.'

—, *Fields, Factories and Workshops* (London: Thomas Nelson, n.d.). Stamped 'J.J.'

*—, *La Granda rivoluzione*   (*James Joyce*, p. 794)

La Motte Fouqué, Friedrich Heinrich Carl de, *Undine* (in English) (London: Edward Lumley, n.d.). Stamped 'J.J.'

Landor, Walter Savage, *Imaginary Conversations* (London, etc.: Walter Scott, n.d. [1895?]). Stamped 'J.J.'

*Langbridge, Frederick, *Ballads and Legends* (London: Routledge, 1903)   (*Critical Writings*, pp. 124–5)

*Latini, Brunetto, *Il Libro delle bestie*   (*James Joyce*, p. 795)

Law, Ernest, *Shakespeare as a Groom of the Chamber* (London: George Bell, 1910)

*Lawrence, D. H., *The Rainbow*   (*Letters*, I. 115)

Lebensbilder unserer Klassiker mit porträts (Berlin, Leipzig: Deutsches Verlagshaus Bong, n.d.)

*Lecky, W. E. H., *History of European Morals*. Purchased 1913–14, Trieste.   (*James Joyce*, p. 788)

Lee, Sidney, *Great Englishmen of the Sixteenth Century* (London: Thomas Nelson, n.d., Preface dated 1907)

Legh, Thomas, *A Narrative of a Journey in Egypt and the Country Beyond the Cataracts* (London: John Murray, 1816)

Leo XIII, *La Poesie Latine*, ed. Gioachimo Pecci (Milan: Sonzogno, n.d.). Stamped 'J.J.' Contains his poem on 'L'Arte fotograficà' mentioned in Joyce's story, 'Grace'.

Leopardi, Giacomo, *Poesie* (Milan: Sonzogno, 1910). Stamped 'J.J.'

*Lermontov, Mikhail Yurevitch, *A Hero of Our Time* (London: Ward and Downey, 1886)   (*Letters*, II. 106, 171)

Le Sage, Alain René, *Gil Blas*, 4 vols., trans. Tobias Smollett (London, 1812)   (*James Joyce*, p. 795)

Lessing, G. E., *The Laocoon and Other Prose Writings*, trans. W. B. Rönnfeldt (London: Walter Scott, n.d.)

Levertin, Oscar, *Epistolario d'Enrico Ibsen*, trans. into Italian B. Carlson and B. Perotti (Locarno: Librairie Internazionale, n.d.). Stamped 'J.J.'

Levides, Pericles, *La Civilisation dans les hopitaux, Les vrais crimes* (no publisher, place or date). Stamped 'J.J.'

Lewis, Wyndham, *Tarr* (London: Egoist Press, 1918). Stamped 'J.J.'   (*Letters*, I. 122)

Leyland, Francis A., *The Brontë Family*, 2 vols. (London: Hurst and Blackett, 1886)

Lie, Jonas, *Niobe*, trans. H. L. Braekstad (London: Heinemann, 1897). Stamped 'J.J.'

—, Østenfor sol (Copenhagen, 1905)   (*James Joyce*, p. 794)

Lingard, John, *History of England*, abridged, with a continuation by James Burke (Dublin: James Duffy, n.d.). Purchased Switzerland.

Literary Year Book, The, ed. Basil Stewart (London: Routledge, 1910). Stamped 'J.J.'

Locke, William J., *The Beloved Vagabond* (London: John Lane, 1914). Purchased Trieste.

Longfellow, Henry Wadsworth, *Hyperion: A Romance* (Boston: Houghton Mifflin, 1882)

—, *Outre-Mer, A Pilgrimage Beyond the Sea* (Boston: Houghton Mifflin, 1883)

Lothar, Rudolph, *Das Wiener Burgtheater* (Berlin and Leipzig: Schuster and Loeffler, n.d. but c. 1904). Stamped 'J.J.'

Loti, Pierre, *The Marriage of Loti*, trans. G. F. Monkshood (London: Siegle, Hill, 1908). Stamped 'J.J.'

—, *Pêcheur d'Islande* (Paris: Calmann-Lévy, n.d.)

Lover, Samuel, ed., *Poems of Ireland* (London: Ward, Lock and Bowden, n.d.)

Lucian, *I Dialoghi degli iddii, dei morti, ed altre opera* ('Il Pescatore', 'L'Icaro menippo', 'Dialogho delle cortigiane', 'Dell'Elettro et de cigni', 'La Trago prodagre') (Milan: Sonzogno, n.d.). Stamped 'J.J.'

Ludovici, Anthony M., *A Defence of Aristocracy* (London: Constable, 1915). Stamped 'J.J.'

*Lustful Acts   (*James Joyce*, p. 794)

Mabinogion, The, trans. Charlotte Guest (London: Dent, Everyman, 1913)

Macaulay, Thomas Babington, *Critical and Historical Essays* (London: Longmans Green, 1874)

Machiavelli, Nicolo, *Mandragola* (Rome: Oreste Garroni, 1910)

Mackenzie, Compton, *The Passionate Elopement* (London: Martin Secker, 1911). Stamped 'J.J.'

Macnamara, Brinsley, *The Valley of the Squinting Windows* (Dublin: Maunsel, 1918). Stamped 'J.J.'

Macpherson, James, *see* Ossian

*Macquoid, Thomas Robert, *Pictures and Legends from Normandy and Brittany*. Possibly *Through Brittany* (London, 1877) and *Through Normandy* (London, 1874). (*James Joyce*, p. 794)

*Maeterlinck, Maurice, *Alladine and Palomides, Interior, The Death of Tintagil*, authorized translation (London, 1899). Signed and dated '1899' by Joyce. (Curran, p.9)

—, *Mary Magdalene*, trans. A. B. de Mattos (London: Methuen, 1912)

*—, *Pelleas and Melisanda, The Sightless*, trans. Laurence Alma Tadema (London, [1895]). Signed and dated '1899' by Joyce.
(Curran, p. 9)
Another copy purchased later.

Magee, W. K., *see* Eglinton, J.

Magrini, Gustavo, *Manuale di musica* (Milan: Ulrico Hoepli, 1916). Stamped 'J.J.'

Maher, Michael, *Psychology* (Manuals of Catholic Philosophy) (New York: Benziger Brothers, n.d.). Stamped 'J.J.'

Maistre, Joseph de, *Oeuvres: Voyage autour de ma chambre etc.* (Paris: Flammarion, n.d.) (Mostly uncut.) Purchased Trieste 1919–20.

Mangan, James Clarence, *Essays in Prose and Verse*, ed. C. P. Meehan (Dublin: James Duffy, 1884). Signed 'Jas A Joyce 1902'.

Mangnall, Richmal, *Historical and Miscellaneous Questions for the Use of Young People* (London: Longman, Rees, Orme, Brown and Green, 1829)

Mann, Heinrich, *Die Armen* (Leipzig: Kurt Wolff, 1917). Stamped 'J.J.'

Manzoni, Alessandro, *Liriche e tragedie*, ed. Luigi Russo (Florence: Sansoni, n.d.)

Marinetti, F. T., et al., *Enquête Internationale sur le vers libre et Manifeste du Futurisme* (Milan: Editions de 'Poesie', 1909)

*Marryat, Frederick, *Peter Simple*   (*Letters*, II. 85)

Martin, Sir Theodore, *see* Gaultier, B.

Martyn, Edward, *The Heather Field* (London: Duckworth, 1917). Stamped 'J.J.'

McCarthy, Michael J. F., *The Irish Revolution* (title page missing [Edinburgh and London: Blackwood, 1912])

*McIntyre, J. Lewis, *Giordano Bruno* (London: Macmillan, 1903)
(*Critical Writings*, pp. 132–4)

*Mason, A. E. W., *The Courtship of Morrice Buckler* (London: Macmillan, 1896)   (*Critical Writings*, pp. 130–1)

*—, *Miranda of the Balcony* (London: Macmillan, 1899)
(*Critical Writings*, pp. 130–1)

*—, *The Philanderers* (London: Macmillan, 1899)
(*Critical Writings*, pp. 130–1)

Massinger, Philip, [*Works*], ed. Arthur Symons (London: Vizetelly, 1889). Stamped 'J.J.'

Maupassant, Guy de, *Boule de suif*, etc. (Paris: Librairie Paul Ollendorff, 1907)

—, *Histoire d'une fille de ferme* (Paris: Flammarion, n.d.)

—, *The Odd Number* [13 Tales], trans. Jonathan Sturges, introduction by Henry James (New York: Harper, 1889). Stamped 'J.J.'

*Melani, *Lettera Italiana* (2 vols.)   (*James Joyce*, p. 794)

*Mercredy, *Map of Ireland*   (*James Joyce*, p. 794)

*Mérimée, Prosper, *Abbé Auban*   (*Letters*. I. 119)

*—, *Carmen*. Purchased Trieste, 1913–14.   (*James Joyce*, p. 788)

Merlin, *The Book of Charms and Ceremonies Whereby All May Have the Opportunity of Obtaining Any Object They Desire* (London: W. Foulsham, 1910). Stamped 'J.J.'

Meyerbeer, Giacomo, *Der Prophet* (Leipzig: Universal Bibliothek, n.d.). Stamped 'J.J.'

Meyrink, Gustav, *Das Grüne Gesicht* (Leipzig: Kurt Wolff, 1917). Stamped 'J.J.'

Michaëlis, Karin, *The Dangerous Age*, with Introduction by Marcel Prévost (London: John Lane, 1912)

Mill, John Stuart, *On Liberty*, with Introduction by W. L. Courtney (London: Walter Scott, n.d.)

Milton, John, *Ode on the Morning of Christ's Nativity, L'Allegro, Il Penseroso and Lycidas*, ed. A. W. Verity (Cambridge University Press, 1911)

Milton, John, *The Poetical Works* (London and Edinburgh: Gall and Englas, n.d.). Stamped 'J.J.'

Minor Elizabethan Drama, The, vol. II: *Pre-Shakespearian Comedies* (London: Dent, Everyman, 1913). Stamped 'J.J.'

*Mirabeau, Comte de, *The Curtain Drawn Up* (*James Joyce*, p. 794)

*Mirbeau, Octave, *Sebastien Roch* (1890)   (*Letters*, II. 202)

Molière, *Théâtre Complet*, 2 vols., ed. Théodore Comte (Paris: Bib. Larousse, n.d.). Purchased Trieste (for 45.60 crowns).
          (*James Joyce*, p. 794)

*Molinari, Luigi, *Il Tramonto del diritto penale* (Milan, 1909)
          (*James Joyce*, p. 794)

*Moore, George, *Celibates: Three Short Stories* (London, 1895)
          (*Letters*, II. 74–5)

—, *Evelyn Innes* (London: T. Fisher Unwin, 1898)
     Another copy (Leipzig: Tauchnitz, 1901)

—, *Hail and Farewell: Ave, Salve, Vale* (Leipzig: Tauchnitz, 1912, 1912, 1914). Each is stamped 'J.J.'

*—, *The Lake* (London: Heinemann, 1905)
          (*Letters*, II. 129, 156, 162–3)

—, *Lewis Seymour and Some Women* (Paris: Louis Conard, 1917)

—, *Memoirs of my Dead Life* (Leipzig: Tauchnitz, 1906). Signed by George Costantini, 1911.

—, *Muslin* (London: Heinemann, 1915). Stamped 'J.J.'

—, *Sister Teresa* (London: T. Fisher Unwin, n.d.)

—, *Spring Days* (Leipzig: Tauchnitz, 1912)

—, *The Untilled Field* (Leipzig: Tauchnitz, 1903). Stamped 'J.J.'
          (*Letters*, II. 71, 111)

*—, *Vain Fortune*, new edition (London: Walter Scott, 1895). Signed 'Jas A Joyce March, 1901'.   (Slocum and Cahoon, p. 177)

Moore, George Foot, *The Literature of the Old Testament* (London: Williams and Norgate, Home University Library, n.d.). Purchased Switzerland.

Moore, Thomas, *Poetical Works* (London: Routledge, n.d.). Stamped 'J.J.'

Moorhouse, E. Hallam, *The Story of Lady Hamilton* (London and Edinburgh: T. N. Foulis, 1911)

Moran, D. P., *Tom O'Kelly* (Dublin: Cahill, James Duffy, 1905). Stamped 'J.J.'

Morris, R., *Specimens of Early English* (Oxford: Clarendon Press, 1867)

*Morrison, Arthur, *Tales of Mean Streets* (London: Methuen, 1894)
(*Letters*, II. 205)

Mozart, W. A., *Die Entführung aus dem Serail* (score) (Leipzig: Universal Bibliothek, n.d.). Stamped 'J.J.'

Murison, A. F., ed., *Selections from the Best English Authors* (Edinburgh: Chambers, 1907). Purchased Trieste.

Murphy, N. J., *The Prophecies of St. Malachy Concerning the Successors of St. Peter to the General Judgment, and the Destiny of Ireland* (no place, publisher, or date)

Murray, Gilbert, *Euripides and His Age* (London: Williams and Norgate, Home University Library, n.d.). Signed by Guido Suppan, 1913.

*Murray, T. C., *Maurice Harte* (Dublin: Maunsel, 1912)
(*James Joyce*, p. 794)

Musset, Alfred de, *La Confession d'un enfant du siècle* (Paris: Bibliothèque Larousse, n.d.). Stamped 'J.J.'

Naylor, Edward W., *Shakespeare and Music* (London: Dent, 1896)

Newman, John Henry, *Essays Critical and Historical*, 2 vols. (London: Longmans Green, 1907)

Nietzsche, Friedrich, *The Birth of Tragedy*, trans. W. A. Haussmann (Edinburgh and London: T. N. Foulis, 1909)

——, *The Case of Wagner, Nietzsche Contra Wagner, Selected Aphorisms*, trans. A. M. Ludovici (Edinburgh and London: T. N. Foulis, 1911)

——, *The Joyful Wisdom*, trans. Thomas Common (London: T. N. Foulis, 1910)

Nievo, I., *Le Confessioni di un ottuagenario*, 2 vols. (Florence: Successori Le Monnier, 1910)

**Nouveau scandale de Londres* (*James Joyce*, p. 794)

O'Brien, R. Barry, *The Life of Charles Stewart Parnell* (London and Edinburgh: Thomas Nelson, [1910?])

O'Duffy, R. J., *Historic Graves in Glasnevin Cemetery* (Dublin: James Duffy, 1915). Stamped 'J.J.'

*Ohnet, Giorgio, *Eva*. Purchased Trieste, 1913–14.
(*James Joyce*, p. 795)

*Ohnet, Giorgio, *La Via della gloria* (*James Joyce*, p. 795)

*O'Kelly, Seamas, *By the Stream of Killmeen* (Dublin and London: 1906) (*Letters*, II. 186)

*Olcott, Henry S., *A Buddhist Catechism according to the Sinhalese Canon* (London: Theosophical Publication Society, [1886?]). Signed 'Jas A Joyce May. 7. 1901'. (Slocum and Cahoon, p. 177)

Olivier, Sydney, *White Capital and Coloured Labour* (Socialist Library) (London: Independent Labour Party, 1906)

Orage, A. R., *An Englishman Talks It Out with an Irishman*, with a Preface by John Eglinton (Dublin: Talbot Press, and London: T. Fisher Unwin, 1918). Stamped 'J.J.'

Ordish, T. F., *Shakespeare's London* (London: Dent, 1904)

*Oriani, Alfredo, *Gelosia*. Purchased Trieste, 1913–14.
(*James Joyce*, p. 788)

O'Shea, Katharine (Mrs. Parnell), *Charles Stewart Parnell*, 2 vols. (London: Cassell, 1914)

Ossian, *Fingal*, trans. into German Reinhold Jachmann (Leipzig: Philipp Reclam, n.d.)

—, *The Poems*, trans. James Macpherson (Leipzig: G. J. Goeschen, 1840). Stamped 'J.J.'

—, *Poesie*, trans. into Italian Melchior Cesarotti, 2 vols. (Bassano, 1819)

Ostrovsky, A. Nicolaivitch, *L'Uragano* (Milan: Sonzogno, n.d.). Stamped 'J.J.'

O'Sullivan, Seumas, *Mud and Purple* (Dublin: Talbot Press, and London: T. Fisher Unwin, 1917). Stamped 'J.J.'

Pagat, Henri, *Discours de M. le Sénateur Triple-Alceste* sur la nécessité de régénérer le mariage qui est l'institution fondamentale de la Société, par l'enseignement officiel de la volupté que le mari doit à la femme et qu'il ignore si souvent l'art de lui procurer (Paris: H. Daragon, 1913). Stamped 'J.J.'

*Palazzeschi, Aldo, *Il Codice di Perelà* (*James Joyce*, p. 794)

Palmer, G. Molyneux, 'O It Was Out by Donnycarny' (manuscript score)

Paolieri, Ferdinando, *Novelle Selvagge* (Milan: Fratelli Treves, 1918). Stamped 'J.J.'

Parnell, Charles Stewart, *Words of the Dead Chief*, compiled by Jennie Wyse-Power (Dublin: Sealy, Bryers and Walker, 1892)

Pater, Walter, *Marius the Epicurean*, vol. I (London: Macmillan, 1911)

—, *The Renaissance* (London: Macmillan, 1912). Signed by Guido Suppan, 1912.

Paul, Herbert Woodfield, *The Life of William Ewart Gladstone* (London: Thomas Nelson, n.d.)

*Payne, George, and James, Rainsford, *The Smuggler*
(*James Joyce*, p. 795)

Peacock, W., ed., *English Prose from Mandeville to Ruskin* (Oxford University Press, World's Classics, 1912)

*Pemberton, Max, *The Sea Wolves* (London: Cassell, 1894)
(*Letters*, II. 82)

Perceval, le Gallois, *The High History of the Holy Graal*, trans. Sebastian Evans (London: Dent, and New York: Dutton, Everyman, 1910)

*Phillips-Wolley, Clive, *see* Wolley, C. P.

Philpotts, Eden, *The Mother* (London: Duckworth, 1913). Stamped 'J.J.'

Pierre de Provence et la Belle Maquelonne, ed. Aldophe Biedermann (Paris: Halle, 1913). Stamped 'J.J.'

Pisacane, Carlo, *Saggi sulla rivoluzione* (Milan: Sonzogno, n.d.)

Plato, *Five Dialogues* bearing on poetic inspiration [*Ion, Symposium, Meno, Phaedro, Phaedrus*] (London: Dent, Everyman, 1913). Stamped 'J.J.'

—, and Zenophon, *Socratic Discourses* (London: Dent, Everyman, 1913). Stamped 'J.J.'

Plutarch, *Lives of Alcibiades and Coriolanus, Aristides and Cato the Censor* (London: Cassell, 1886)

*—, *Morals: Theosophical Essays*, trans. C. W. King (London: George Bell, 1882). Contains 'On Isis and Osiris', 'On the Cessation of Oracles', 'On the Pythian Responses', 'On the ε at Delphi', 'On the Apparent Face in the Orb of the Moon', 'On Superstition.' Stamped 'J.J.'   (At Buffalo)

Pocket Missal, The, ed. Father Aloysius (Dublin: M. H. Gill, n.d.). Signed Ken Monaghan.

Poe, Edgar Allan, *Tales*, ed. John H. Ingram (Leipzig: Tauchnitz, 1884). Stamped 'J.J.'

Poggio, *Facezie* (Lanciano: Carabba Editore, n.d.)

*Pollock, John, *The Popish Plot* (London: Duckworth, 1903)
(*Critical Writings*, pp. 119–20)

Polti, Georges, *Les Trente-six situations dramatiques* (Paris: Mercure de France, 1912). Stamped 'J.J.'

Porter, J. L., *The Giant Cities of Bashan* (London: Thomas Nelson, 1865). Stamped 'J.J.'

Pound, Ezra, *Lustra* (privately printed, [1916]) (No. 11 out of 200 copies). Stamped 'J.J.'

—, *Personae and Exaltations* (London: Elkin Mathews, 1913). Stamped 'J.J.'

—, *Ripostes* (London: Elkin Mathews, 1915). Stamped 'J.J.'

—, *Sonnets and Ballate of Guido Cavalcanti* (London: Stephen Swift, 1912). Stamped 'J.J.'

—, and Fenollosa, Ernest, *'Noh' or Accomplishment* (New York: Knopf, 1917). Inscribed to Joyce by John Quinn, 29 June 1917.

Praga, Marco, *Alleluja* (Milan: Baldini, 1904)

(*James Joyce*, p. 794)

*—, *La Biondina* (*James Joyce*, p. 794)

—, *L'Erede* (Milan: Baldini, 1906 and 1914). Two copies.

—, *L'Innamorata* (Milan: Baldini, 1906)

—, *La Moglie ideale* (*James Joyce*, p. 794)

—, *La Porta chiusa, L'Erede* (Milan: Fratelli Treves, 1914)

—, *Storie di palcoscenico* (Milan: Baldini, 1905)

—, *Le Vergini* (Milan: Baldini, 1906) (*James Joyce*, p. 794)

Proudhon., P. J., *Qu'est-ce que la propriété* (Paris: A. Lacroix, 1873)

Purcell, Henry, *see* Runciman, J. F.

Quackenbos, John Duncan, *Practical Rhetoric* (New York: American Book Company, 1896). Stamped 'J.J.'

Quintillian, *Unterricht in der Beredsamkeit*, Book X, trans. into German W. Nicolai (Leipzig: Universal Bibliothek, n.d.). Stamped 'J.J.' Purchased Switzerland.

Rabelais, François, *Les Cinq livres*, 2 vols. (Paris: Flammarion, n.d.)

Rait, R. S., *Life in the Medieval University* (Cambridge University Press, 1912)

Raleigh, Walter, *Shakespeare* (London: Macmillan, 1911)

Ramacharaka [Yogi], *Fourteen Lessons in Yogi Philosophy and Oriental Occultism* (Chicago: Yogi Publication Society, 1903). Stamped 'J.J.'

Rawson, Maud Stepney, *Penelope Rich and Her Circle* (London: Hutchinson, 1911). Stamped 'J.J.'

Redmond, John, *What the Irish Regiments Have Done* (London: T. Fisher Unwin, 1916). Stamped 'J.J.'

Reid, Forrest, *Following Darkness* (London: Edward Arnold, 1912). Stamped 'J.J.' (*Letters*, II. 395)

Renan, Ernest, *The Life of Jesus* (London: Watts, 1913). Stamped 'J.J.' (*Letters*, II. 76)

—, *Souvenirs d'enfance et de jeunesse* (Paris: Calmann-Lévy, 1883). Inscribed 'J A J Pola, Austria 1904'. (*Letters*, II. 72)

Renard, Jules, *Le Coureur de filles* (Paris: Flammarion, n.d.)

—, *Poil de carrotte* (Paris: Calmann-Lévy, n.d.)

Rey, Albert, *Skelton's Satiric Poems in Their Relation to Lydgate . . .* (Bern: K. J. Wyss, 1899). Stamped 'J.J.'

*Ricard, Xavier de, *Der Zorn* (*James Joyce*, p. 794)

*Rickaby, Joseph, *Of God and His Creatures*, an annotated translation of the *Summa Contra Gentiles* of Thomas Aquinas (1905). Purchased Trieste, 1913–14. (*James Joyce*, p. 788)

Riley, William, *Windyridge* (London: Herbert Jenkins [1915?]). Probably purchased 1915.

*Rita [pseudonym of E. M. J. Humphreys], *Mrs. Hypocrite* (London: Hutchinson, 1897) (*Letters*, II. 83)

*Robinson, Lennox, *Patriots* (Dublin: Maunsel, 1912) (*James Joyce*, p. 794)

*Rooney, William, *Poems and Ballads*, ed. Arthur Griffith (Dublin: United Irishman, [1902]) (*Critical Writings*, pp. 84–7)

Rousseau, Jean-Jacques, *Les Confessions*, 2 vols. (Paris: Flammarion, n.d.)

Runciman, John F., *Purcell* (London: George Bell, 1909)

—, *Wagner* (London: George Bell, 1905)

*Ruskin, John, *Mornings in Florence* (London: George Allen, 4th ed., 1894). Signed 'Jas. A. Joyce September 9th 1898'. Photocopy of inscribed title-page in the National Library of Ireland.

Russell, Bertrand, *Principles of Social Reconstruction* (London: George Allen and Unwin, 1917)

*Russell, T. Baron, *Borlase and Son* (London: John Lane, 1903) (*Critical Writings*, pp. 139–40)

Rutherford, Mark, *The Autobiography of* (London: T. Fisher Unwin, n.d., 15th edition). Stamped 'J.J.'

Sacher, H., ed., *Zionism and the Jewish Future* (London: John Murray, 1916). Stamped 'J.J.'

*Sacher-Masoch, Leopold von, *Grausame Frauen*, 4 vols.

(*James Joyce*, p. 794)

*—, *Katharina II* (Berlin, n.d.)   (*James Joyce*, p. 794)

—, *Liebesgeschichten* (Berlin, n.d.)   (*James Joyce*, p. 794)

*—, *Scene del ghetto*   (*James Joyce*, p. 794)

Sacra Bibbia, La (Italian Bible) (Rome, 1912). Stamped 'J.J.'

Saintsbury, George, *A Short History of English Literature* (London: Macmillan, 1908)

—, *A History of English Prose Rhythm* (London: Macmillan, 1912)

*Sauer, *Englische Grammatik*. Purchased Trieste, 1913–14.

(*James Joyce*, p. 788)

Schickele, René, *Hans in Schnakenloch* (Leipzig: Verlag der Weissen Bücher, 1915). Stamped 'J.J.'

*Schiller, F. C. S., *Humanism: Philosophical Essays* (London: Macmillan, 1903)   (*Critical Writings*, pp. 135–6)

*Schlüssel, *Englische Grammatik*. Purchased Trieste, 1913–14.

(*James Joyce*, p. 788)

Schnitzler, Arthur, *Lieutenant Gustl* (Berlin: S. Fischer, 1906)

Schopenhauer, Arthur, *Essays*, trans. Mrs. Rudolf Dircks (*London*: Walter Scott, n.d.)

Scott, Walter, *The Bride of Lammermoor* (Leipzig: Tauchnitz, 1858)

Seeley, John R., *Ecce Homo* [life of Christ] (London: Thomas Nelson, n.d.). Stamped 'J.J.'

Shakespeare, William, *As You Like It* (Leipzig: Tauchnitz, 1868). Stamped 'J.J.'

—, *Cymbeline* (Leipzig: Tauchnitz, 1868). Stamped 'J.J.'

—, *Doubtful Plays of* (Leipzig: Tauchnitz, 1896). Stamped 'J.J.'

—, *Hamlet*, ed. K. Deighton (London: Macmillan, 1910)

—, *Hamlet*, ed. A. W. Verity (Cambridge University Press, 1911)

—, *Henry IV, Part I* (Leipzig: Tauchnitz, 1868). Stamped 'J.J.'

—, *Henry IV, Part II* (Leipzig: Tauchnitz, 1868). Stamped 'J.J.'

—, *Julius Caesar*, ed. A. W. Verity (Cambridge University Press, 1910)

—, *King Lear*, ed. A. W. Verity (Cambridge University Press, 1908)

—, *A List of All the Songs and Passages in Shakespeare which have been set to music*, compiled by J. Greenhill, W. A. Harrison, F. J. Furnivall (London: New Shakespeare Society, 1884)

—, *Macbeth* (Leipzig: Tauchnitz, 1868). Stamped 'J.J.'

—, *Macbeth*, ed. A. W. Verity (Cambridge University Press, 1909)

—, *A Midsummer Night's Dream*, ed. A. W. Verity (Cambridge University Press, 1908). Purchased Trieste.

—, *Much Ado About Nothing* (Leipzig: Tauchnitz, 1868). Stamped 'J.J.'

—, *Othello* (Leipzig: Tauchnitz, 1868). Stamped 'J.J.'

—, *Richard III* (Leipzig: Tauchnitz, 1868). Stamped 'J.J.'

—, *Romeo and Juliet*, ed. K. Deighton (London: Macmillan, 1912)

—, *The Taming of the Shrew* (Leipzig: Tauchnitz, 1868). Stamped 'J.J.'

—, *Troilus and Cressida* (Leipzig: Tauchnitz, 1868). Stamped 'J.J.'

—, *The Two Noble Kinsmen* (attributed to Shakespeare), ed. C. H. Herford (London, Dent, 1897). Stamped 'J.J.'

—, *The Works*, ed. by the editor of the 'Chandos' classics ('Universal' Editions) (London: Frederick Warne, 1890). Stamped 'J.J.'

—, *see also* Alvor, Bormann, Brandes, Clare, Hazlitt, Jameson, Law, Lee, Naylor, Ordish, Raleigh, Rawson, Wilson

*Sharp, Cecil James, *A Book of British Song for Home and School* (London: John Murray, 1902)   (*Letters*, II. 21)

Shaw, Bernard, *Cashel Byron's Profession* (Leipzig: Tauchnitz, 1914)

—, *The Devil's Disciple* (London, Constable, 1913). Purchased Trieste 1913–14.   (*James Joyce*, p. 788)

—, *Getting Married* and *The Shewing-Up of Blanco Posnet* (Leipzig: Tauchnitz, 1914)

—, *John Bull's Other Island* (London: Constable, 1909). Purchased Trieste.

—, *Love among the Artists* (London: Constable, 1914). Stamped 'J.J.'

—, *Major Barbara* (London: Constable, 1912). Purchased Trieste.   (*James Joyce*, p. 788)

—, *Misalliance, The Dark Lady of the Sonnets*, and *Fanny's First Play*, with a Treatise on Parents and Children (London: Constable, 1914). Stamped 'J.J.' For *The Dark Lady*, see *Critical Writings*, p. 250.

—, *Mrs. Warren's Profession* (London: Constable, 1907)   (*Letters*, II. 453)

Shaw, Bernard, *The Perfect Wagnerite* (Leipzig: Tauchnitz, 1913)

—, *The Philanderer* (London: Constable, 1910)

—, *The Shewing-Up of Blanco Posnet* (*Critical Writings*, pp. 206–8)

—, *Socialism and Superior Brains* (London: A. C. Fifield, 1910)

—, *The Three Unpleasant Plays* [*Widower's Houses*, *The Philanderer*, *Mrs. Warren's Profession*] (Leipzig: Tauchnitz, 1914)

Sheehy Skeffington, Francis, *In Dark and Evil Days* (Dublin: James Duffy, 1916). Stamped 'J.J.'

Shelley, Percy Bysshe, *The Complete Poetical Works*, ed. Thomas Hutchinson (London: Oxford University Press, 1912). Purchased Trieste.

—, *The Poetical Works* (London: Milner and Sowerby, n.d.). Stamped 'J.J.'

Sherard, Robert H., *Oscar Wilde* (London: Greening, 1908)

Sickert, Bernhard, *Whistler* (London: Duckworth, n.d.). Stamped 'J.J.'

Sienkiewicz, Henryk, *Quo Vadis* (Boston: Little Brown, 1892)

Skelton, John, *see* Rey, A.

Smaller Classical Dictionary, A, ed. E. H. Blakeney (London: Dent, and New York: Dutton, 1917). Signed Guido Suppan, 1919 and S. Joyce, 1933.

Smith, Charles John, *Synonyms Discriminated*, ed. H. Percy Smith (London: George Bell, 1913). Stamped 'J.J.'

Smollett, Tobias, *Humphry Clinker* (London: George Bell, 1917) (Bohn's Library)

—, *Roderick Random* (London: George Bell, 1915) (Bohn's Library)

—, *see also* Le Sage, A. R.

Solomon, Joseph, *Bergson* (London: Constable, 1912)

Spencer, Herbert, *The Study of Sociology* (London: Kegan Paul Trench, 1888). Purchased Trieste 1919–20.

Steed, Henry Wickham, *The Hapsburg Monarchy* (London: Constable, 1913)

Steiner, Rudolf, *Blut ist ein ganz besonderer Saft* (Berlin: Philosophisch-Theosophischer Verlag, 1910). Stamped 'J.J.'

Stephens, James, *Here Are Ladies* (Leipzig: Tauchnitz, 1913)

—, *Insurrections* (Dublin: Maunsel, 1909)

Sterne, Laurence, *The Life and Opinions of Tristram Shandy, Gentleman* (Oxford University Press, World's Classics, 1903)

—, *A Sentimental Journey* (London: Routledge, 1888). Signed by Henry N. Blackwood Price.

Stevenson, Robert Louis, *Catriona* (Leipzig: Tauchnitz, 1893)

Stewart, Basil, see *Literary Year-Book, The*

Strindberg, August, *The Confession of a Fool*, trans. Ellie Schleussner (London: Stephen Swift, 1912). Purchased Trieste.

—, *Fräulein Julie*, trans. into German E. Brausewetter (Leipzig: Universal Bibliothek, n.d.)

—, *Gläubiger*, trans. into German Erich Holm (Leipzig: Universal Bibliothek, n.d.). Stamped 'J.J.'

—, *Der Vater* (Leipzig: Universal Bibliothek, n.d.). Stamped 'J.J.'

*Sudermann, Hermann, *Dame Care*   (*Letters*, II. 25)

—, *The Undying Past*, trans. Beatrice Marshall (London: John Lane, 1906). Stamped 'J.J.'

Sue, Eugène, *Le Juif errant* (Paris: Artheme Fayard, n.d.). Purchased Trieste.

Summers, W. H., *The Lollards of the Chiltern Hills* (London: Frances Griffiths, 1906). Stamped 'J.J.'

Svevo, Italo, *Senilità* (Trieste: Ettore Vram, 1898)

—, *Una Vita* (Trieste: Ettore Vram, 1893)

Swedenborg, Emanuel, *Heaven and Its Wonders and Hell* (London: Swedenborg Society, 1905)

Swift, Jonathan, *A Tale of a Tub, The Battle of the Books and Other Satires* (London: Dent, Everyman, 1916). Stamped 'J.J.'

—, *Travels into Several Remote Nations of the World, by Lemuel Gulliver* (New York: Frank E. Lovell, n.d.). Stamped 'J.J.'

—, *The Works*, with a biography by D. Laing Purves (Edinburgh: William P. Nimmo, 1869)

Swinburne, Algernon Charles, *Atalanta in Calydon and Lyrical Poems* (Leipzig: Tauchnitz, 1901)

Symons, Arthur, *Cities of Italy* (London: Dent, 1907). Inscribed, presumably by Symons, 'James Joyce with many wishes for a happy Xmas 1910'.

*—, *The Symbolist Movement in Literature* (London: Heinemann, 1899)
                                        (*Letters*, II. 173)

Synge, J. M., *The Aran Islands* (Dublin: Maunsel, 1907). Purchased Trieste.

—, *The Playboy of the Western World* (Dublin: Maunsel, 1907). Purchased Trieste.

Synge, J. M., *The Shadow of the Glen* and *Riders to the Sea* (London: Elkin Mathews, 1907)
>   (*Critical Writings*, p. 250; *Letters*, I. 66–7, 95, 117)
—, *The Tinker's Wedding* (Dublin: Maunsel, 1907)
—, *The Well of the Saints* (Dublin: Maunsel, 1907)

**Tabernacle and the Church, The*, catechetically explained (London, 1859)   (*James Joyce*, p. 794)

Tacitus, *La Germania*, trans. into Italian Emilio Amadeo (Milan: Signorelli, n.d.)

Tennyson, Alfred, *Enoch Arden*, etc. (London: Edward Moxon, 1864)

—, *The Poetical Works* (Boston: James R. Osgood, 1872)

—, *Selections*, ed. with notes by F. J. Rowe and W. T. Webb (London: Macmillan, 1889)

Thackeray, William Makepeace, *The History of Henry Esmond, Esq.* (London: Thomas Nelson, n.d.)

—, *Vanity Fair* (London: Thomas Nelson, 1890)

Thomas, Edward, *Richard Jefferies, His Life and Work* (London: Hutchinson, [1909]). Stamped 'J.J.' Purchased Zurich.

*Thurston, E. Temple, *The Realist* (London: Sisley's, 1906; John Lane, 1914)   (*Letters*, II. 205)

*Tinayre, Marcelle, *The House of Sin*, trans. A. Smyth (London: Maclaren, 1903)   (*Critical Writings*, pp. 121–3)

*Tolstoy, Leo, *Anna Karenina*   (*Letters*, II. 107)

*—, *Essays and Letters*, trans. Aylmer Maude (London, etc.: Henry Frowde, 1904). Stamped 'J.J.'   (At Buffalo)

*—, *The Fruits of Enlightenment*, trans. E. J. Dillon, with Introduction by Arthur Wing Pinero (London: Heinemann, 1891). Inscribed 'Jas A Joyce April 1901'.   (Slocum and Cahoon, p. 177)

*—, *Pensieri di saggi per ogni giorno* (1908)   (*James Joyce*, p. 794)
—, *La Potenza delle tenebre* (Naples: Salvatore Romano, 1905)

—, *Resurrection*, trans. Louise Maude (London: Constable, n.d. but Preface dated 1910). Stamped 'J.J.'   (*Letters*, II. 82)

*—, *Der Roman der Ehe*   (*James Joyce*, p. 794)

—, *Saggi: Agli Uomini politici, La Guerra Russo-Giapponese*, trans. into Italian Maria Salvi (Milan: Sonzogno, 1911)

—, *La Sonata a Kreutzer* (no publisher, n.d.)

—, *Usseri: Un Incontro al Caucaso* (Milan: Sonzogno, 1902)

Treble, H. A., compiler, *English Prose* (Oxford University Press, World's Classics, 1917). Purchased Trieste, 1919–20.

Trench, Richard Chevenix, *Proverbs and Their Lessons* (London: Macmillan, 1869). Stamped 'J.J.'

Tschudi, Clara, *Ludwig the Second*, trans. E. H. Hearn (London: Swan Sonnenschein, 1908)

*Tucker, Benjamin, R., *Instead of a Book* (New York: Benjamin R. Tucker, 1897). Stamped 'J.J.' (At Buffalo)

Turgenev, Ivan, Works in 11 volumes (London: Heinemann, 1910–13):
    The Diary of a Superfluous Man, etc. (1913)
    Dream Tales and Prose Poems, trans. C. Garnett (1913)
    Fathers and Children (1913)
    The Jew, etc. (1913)
    A Lear of the Steppes, etc. (1912) (*Letters*, II. 90)
    On the Eve (1911)
    Smoke (1910). Purchased Trieste, 1913–14
                               (*James Joyce*, p. 788; *Letters*, II. 207)
    A Sportsman's Sketches, 2 vols. (1913) (*Letters*, II. 207)
    Virgin Soil, 2 vols. (1913) (*James Joyce*, p. 794)

Twain, Mark, *The New Pilgrim's Progress* (London: John Camden Hotten, n.d.) (pp. 195–200 on Wandering Jew)

Udall, Nicholas, *Roister Doister* (London: Constable, 1898). Stamped 'J.J.'

Valera, Juan, *Don Braulio*, trans. Clara Bell (New York: Appleton, 1892). Stamped 'J.J.'

*Verlaine, Paul, *Les Poètes maudits* (Paris, 1900). Signed 'J.A.J. 1902'. (Curran, p. 9)

Virgil, *Eneide*, trans. into Italian Alfredo Baroli (Milan: Signorelli, n.d.) Books I, II, III, IV in separate volumes

—, *Le Georgiche*, interlinear translation into Italian (Milan, etc.: Albrighi, Segati, 1915)

—, *Opera*, ed. E. Benoist and M. Duvau (Paris: Hachette, 1915). Stamped 'J.J.'

Voltaire, *History of Charles XII*, trans. Winifred Todhunter (London: Dent, n.d.)

—, *Oeuvres choisies* [poems] (Avignon: A. Giroud, 1761)

Voss, Paul, *Georges Bizet* (Leipzig: Universal Bibliothek, n.d.) Stamped 'J.J.'

—, *Vincenzo Bellini* (Leipzig: Universal Bibliothek, n.d.)

Wagner, Richard, *Der Fliegende Holländer* (score) (Leipzig: Universal Bibliothek, n.d.). Stamped 'J.J.'

—, *Götterdämmerung* (Mainz: B. Schott's Söhne, [1919?]). Stamped 'J.J.'

—, *Judaism in Music*, trans. Edwin Evans (London: William Reeves, 1910)

—, *Letters to August Roeckel*, trans. E. C. Sellar (Bristol: Arrowsmith, n.d.). Introductory essay by Houston Chamberlain.

—, *Die Meistersinger* (*Letters*, I. 67)

*—, *Operas* (*Letters*, II. 25)

—, *Prose Works* ('Art and Revolution', 'The Art-Work of the Future', 'Wieland the Smith', 'Art and Climate', 'A Communication to My Friends'), trans. W. A. Ellis, vol. I (London: Kegan Paul, Trench, Trübner, 1892)

—, *Das Rheingold* (score) (Leipzig: Philipp Reclam, n.d.). Stamped 'J.J.'

—, *Richard to Minna Wagner* [Letters], ed. and trans. W. A. Ellis, 2 vols. (London: H. Grevel, 1909)

—, *Siegfried* (score) (Mainz: B. Schott's Söhne, n.d.). Stamped 'J.J.'

—, *see also* May Byron, Golther, Runciman

Walshe, R. G., *Knocknagow* (Dublin: James Duffy, 1917). Stamped 'J.J.' (A play based on Charles J. Kickham's novel.)

Ward, A. W., *Chaucer*, ed. John Morley (London: Macmillan, 1893)

Warren, Kate M., *A Treasury of English Literature*, with Introduction by Stopford A. Brooke (London: Constable, 1908)

Webb, Sidney, and Sidney Ball, G. Bernard Shaw, Sir Oliver Lodge, *Socialism and Individualism* (Fabian Socialist Series No. 3) (London: A. C. Fifield, 1909)

Wedekind, Frank, *Die Büchse der Pandora* (Berlin: Bruno Cassirer, n.d., but previous owner has signed with date December 1907)

*—, *Die Zensur* (Berlin, 1908) (*James Joyce*, p. 794)

Wells, H. G., *Bealby* (Paris: Louis Conard, 1915). Stamped 'J.J.'

—, *The History of Mr. Polly* (London: Thomas Nelson, n.d.). Stamped 'J.J.' Purchased Zurich.

—, *Kipps* (London: Thomas Nelson, n.d.)

—, *A Modern Utopia* (Leipzig: Tauchnitz, 1905). Previous owner was Giulio Veneziani, a relative of Svevo.

Werfel, Franz, *Die Troierinnen des Euripedes* (Leipzig: Kurt Wolff, 1916). Stamped 'J.J.'

Whitman, Walt, *Democratic Vistas* (London: Routledge, and New York: Dutton, n.d.)

—, *Leaves of Grass* (New York and London: Appleton, 1912). Stanislaus Joyce has signed his name.

Wilde, Oscar, *An Ideal Husband* (Leipzig: Tauchnitz, 1907)

—, *Intentions* (Leipzig: English Library, 1907)

—, *Lady Windermere's Fan* (Leipzig: Tauchnitz, 1909). Signed by S. Joyce.

—, *The Picture of Dorian Gray* (Leipzig: Tauchnitz, 1908)
(*Letters*, II. 149–50)

—, *Salome* (Leipzig: Tauchnitz, 1909)

—, *Selected Poems* (London: Methuen, 1911)

—, *The Soul of Man under Socialism* (London: Privately printed, 1904)

—, *A Woman of No Importance* (Leipzig: Tauchnitz, 1909)

—, *see also* Sherard, R. H.

Wilson, John Dover, compiler, *Life in Shakespeare's England, A Book of Elizabethan Prose* (Cambridge University Press, 1911). Purchased Trieste.

*Witt, C., *Myths of Hellas or Greek Tales*, trans Francis Younghusband (London: Longmans, 1883). Stamped 'J.J.'   (At Buffalo)

*Wolley, Clive Phillips, *Songs of an English Esau* (London: Smith, Elder, 1902)   (*Critical Writings*, p. 97)

Wood, J. G., *Common Objects of the Seashore* (London: Routledge, 1912). Stamped 'J.J.'

Woolf, Virginia, *The Voyage Out* (London: Duckworth, 1915). Stamped 'J.J.'   (*Letters*, I. 105)

Woolley, Edward Mott, *The Art of Selling Goods* (Chicago: American Business Man, 1907). Stamped 'J.J.'

Yeats, John Butler, *Essays Irish and American* (Dublin and London: T. Fisher Unwin, 1918). Stamped 'J.J.'

*Yeats, William Butler, *The Countess Cathleen* (London: T. Fisher Unwin, 1912)   (*Letters*, I. 71)

—, *The Hour-Glass* (London: A. H. Bullen, 1907). Purchased Trieste.

—, *Ideas of Good and Evil* (Dublin: Maunsel, 1905)

*—, *John Sherman: and, Dhoya* (London: T. Fisher Unwin, 1891). Signed 'Jas A Joyce [1902]'.   (Slocum and Cahoon, p. 178)

—, *The Land of Heart's Desire* (London: T. Fisher Unwin, 1912)
(*James Joyce*, p. 794)

—, *The Tables of the Law* and *The Adoration of the Magi* (London: Elkin Mathews, 1904)

Young, Filson, *The Sands of Pleasure* (London: Grant Richards, 1908)

Zola, Emile, *La Débacle*, 2 vols. (Paris: Bibliothèque-Charpentier, 1912)

—, *Nana*, 3 unbound volumes (Paris: Editions Parisiennes, n.d.)

Notes

Introduction

p. 1
'Intensities' and 'Bullockships'   'A Portrait of the Artist', in *The Workshop of Daedalus*, ed. Robert Scholes and Richard M. Kain (Evanston, Ill., 1965), p. 67.

p. 2
'a loathsome brood of apostates'   *Freeman's Journal*, 10 May 1899.

p. 3
Remembering how Balzac . . .   See B. Guyon, *La Création littéraire chez Balzac* (Paris, 1951), pp. 66–76.

choice of the engineer . . .   Jacques Mercanton, *Les Heures de James Joyce* (Lausanne, 1967), p. 42, and 'James Joyce', *Europe*, no. 184 (15 Apr. 1938), p. 439.

'Imagination is . . . what is remembered'   Giambattista Vico, *The New Science*, trans. T. G. Bergin and M. H. Fisch (Ithaca, N.Y., 1968), no. 699. Cf. nos. 211 and 819, and also Joyce's remark that 'imagination is memory' in Frank Budgen, *Myselves When Young* (London, 1970), p. 187.

p. 4
He would later detect in Shakespeare . . .   *Ulysses*, p. 212 (272).

'I don't like music . . .'   Louis Gillet, *Claybook for James Joyce*, ed. Georges Markow-Totevy (London and New York, 1958), p. 109.

disqualified . . . by 'vigour of the mind'   *The Workshop of Daedalus*, p. 96.

p. 5
'mathematics for ladies'   The *Lestrygonians* notebook is in the Lockwood Memorial Library, State University of New York at Buffalo.

rose pattern . . . in the steel dust   Ezra Pound, *Cantos*, 2d ed. (London, 1964), Canto LXXIV.

p. 7
In fiction the principal names . . .   Joyce did not keep his copies of Henry James's works, but that he read several of them is proved by his letters. See headnote to Appendix, p. 97.

p. 8

(*as several critics have surmised*)   See A. Walton Litz, 'Ithaca', in *James Joyce's* Ulysses, ed. Clive Hart and David Hayman (Berkeley, Calif., 1974), p. 394.

Chapter I HOMER

The principal works on Homer and Joyce are W. B. Stanford, *The Ulysses Theme* (Oxford, 1963) and Stuart Gilbert, *James Joyce's 'Ulysses'*, 2nd ed. (New York, 1952). As Joyce's manuscripts and preliminary notes are deciphered by Phillip F. Herring and others, evidence has accumulated of Joyce's careful reading of Bérard, Roscher, and others. See, for example, Herring, '*Ulysses* Notebook VIII.A.5 at Buffalo', *Studies in Bibliography*, 22 (1969), pp. 287–310.

p. 10

'*Ancient salt is best packing*'   W. B. Yeats, *Essays and Introductions* (London and New York, 1961), p. 522.

'*an afterthought of Europe*'   *Stephen Hero*, p. 53, and Notebook in Herbert Gorman, *James Joyce* (New York, 1939), p. 135.

This anastomosis of antiquity . . .   The comparison of Harry Richmond to both Ulysses and Telemachus is well treated in Barbara Hardy, 'The Structure of Imagery: George Meredith's *Harry Richmond*', in *The Appropriate Form* (London, 1971), pp. 83–104.

p. 11

cast in the heroic mould   *Letters*, II. 108. Cf. the view of modern heroism in 'Drama and Life', *The Critical Writings of James Joyce*, ed. Ellsworth G. Mason and Richard Ellmann (London and New York, 1959), p. 45.

p. 13

'*Why do you odysseus him so* . . .'   G. E. Dimock, 'The Name of Ulysses', in *The Odyssey*, trans. and ed. Albert Cook (New York, 1974), p. 409.

'*big ears descended from Zeus*'   W. N. Roscher, *Ausführliches Lexikon der Griechischen und Römischen Mythologie* (Leipzig, 1897–1902), III. 651.

p. 17

Ulysses was praised . . .   T. S. Eliot, '*Ulysses*, Order, and Myth', *The Dial*, LXXV (1923), pp. 480–3.

It was not . . . '*two plane*'   Quoted in Joyce, *Letters*, II. 83.

p. 19

The relationship to Peer Gynt . . .   See also B. J. Tysdahl, *Joyce and*

Ibsen (Oslo and New York, 1968), and Kristian Smidt's comments on the book in 'Joyce and Ibsen: A Study in Literary Influence', *Edda*, Hefte 2 (1970), which discusses other criticism of this relationship.

'extravagant excursions into forbidden territory'   Compare the epigraph to *A Portrait*, *'Et ignotas animum dimittit in artes'* (from Ovid's *Metamorphoses*, VIII. 188). Joyce omits the following phrase, *'naturamque novat'*, for he does not believe that the artist changes nature's laws.

p. 20
in December 1902 he quotes Gretchen's song . . .   *Letters*, II. 24.

Mephistopheles is the spirit of denial . . .   Stuart Atkins, *Goethe's Faust* (Cambridge, Mass., 1958), p. 41.

p. 21
Ewig-Leere . . . Ewig-Weibliche   *Faust*, Part Two, 11. 11603, 12110.

p. 22
'Psychologist! What can a man know . . .'   Richard Ellmann, *James Joyce* (New York and London, 1959), p. 275.

p. 23
She complained to Frank Budgen . . .   *Myselves When Young*, p. 188.

'He was after all only a literary man . . .'   Samuel Butler, *The Humour of Homer* (London, 1913), p. 60.

p. 24
to Vladimir Nabokov . . . *he disclaimed* . . .   Alfred Appel, Jr., writes me of Nabokov's conversation with him in July 1974: 'VN recalled a dinner conversation with Joyce at the apartment of the Léons, Paris, ca. 1937. Joyce said something disparaging about the use of mythology in modern literature. Amazed, Nabokov said, "But you employed Homer!" "A whim," answered Joyce. "But you collaborated with Gilbert," persisted Nabokov. "A terrible mistake," replied Joyce. " 'An advertisement for the book. I regret it very much,' Joyce told me. I hear him so clearly, right now—that reedy, beautiful voice," says Nabokov, staring into the middle distance, his inner ear finely tuned to that music by the perfect pitch of memory.'

p. 25
'Perhaps, in fact, he does give less thought . . .'   Ellmann, *James Joyce*, p. 731.

p. 27
the doublet . . . *Phoenician sailing manual*   Victor Bérard, *Les Phéniciens et l'Odyssée*, 2 vols. (Paris, 1902–3), I. 50; II. 264; also Bérard, *Did Homer Live?* (London, 1931), p. 120.

p. 30
joining of Penelope and Telegonus . . .   Aristotle and others report that
Telemachus married Nausicaa. Molly Bloom's passing interest in
Stephen is a kind of summary of all these erotic possibilities involving
Calypso, Nausicaa, Circe, and Penelope.

p. 33
'perhaps baldheaded'   Ellmann, *James Joyce*, p. 430.

'the parts that mattered'   Frank Budgen, *James Joyce and the Making of
Ulysses* (London, 1972), p. 17.

p. 34
Joyce's developing interest in the Jews   See Louis Hyman, *The Jews of
Ireland* (Shannon, 1972), for a valuable treatment of this subject.

p. 35
The Language of the Outlaw   I am grateful to Ellsworth G. Mason
for a copy of this pamphlet.

p. 39
Homer was not a delicate writer   Vico, *La Scienza nuova*, no. 822.

a belligerent situation . . . suited to epic   G. W. F. Hegel, *Aesthetics*, trans.
T. M. Knox (Oxford, 1975), II. 1059.

p. 42
moly . . . *signifies everything*   For *moly* see A. Walton Litz, *The Art of
James Joyce* (London, 1961), pp. 25–6.

p. 44
'There is no subjectivity whatever . . .'   Cf. Arthur Power, *Conversations
with James Joyce* (London, 1974), p. 74.

Chapter II SHAKESPEARE

p. 46
'Il n'y a qu'une feuille qui sépare . . .'   Mercanton, *Les Heures de
James Joyce*, p. 26.

p. 48
'Talk to me of originality . . .'   Yeats, 'A General Introduction to
My Work', in *Essays and Introductions*, p. 522.

twelve lectures . . . in Trieste in 1912–13   The lectures, originally
intended to be ten in number, eventually became twelve. The
following notices of them (translated here into English) appeared in
the *Piccolo della Sera*.

9 November 1912 (p. 3)
    The Minerva society management has arranged for its members
to attend, at half the usual admission price, the lectures on Shake-

speare that Professor James Joyce will deliver in the social hall. He
proposes to explain *Hamlet* in English in a course of ten lectures on
successive Monday evenings at 8.15, beginning 11 November.
Advance bookings can be made at the social office, via Giosuè
Carducci 28.

12 November 1912 (p. 3)

The First Joyce Lecture. In the Minerva hall, which was completely
full, Professor James Joyce, whom our intellectual community knows
and respects as thinker, man of culture, and freelance writer, began
yesterday his series of ten lectures on Shakespeare's *Hamlet* with an
introductory lecture that, by its dense yet clear concepts, by a form
as noble as it was simple, and by wit and vivacity, achieved a
genuine brilliance. In his lecture Professor Joyce began with a con-
cise exposition of the origins of the drama, passed on to a colourful
presentation of the writers in the age of Elizabeth, and finally out-
lined the character and life of Shakespeare with particular attention
to the psychological moment when he wrote *Hamlet*. Warm and
prolonged applause greeted the speaker at the end of his learned and
graceful talk.

The second lecture will take place next Monday. In it Professor
Joyce will begin his reading and commentary on *Hamlet*.

1 December 1912 (p. 4)

Joyce Lecture. Tomorrow evening at 8.15, in the Minerva hall,
Professor James Joyce will give the third lecture of his series on
Shakespeare's *Hamlet*.

11 February 1913 (p. 2)

Dr. James Joyce's Lectures. Yesterday evening Dr. James Joyce concluded his series of lectures in English on *Hamlet*. The hall was well
attended during all twelve lectures. The English colony appeared to
be thinly or not at all represented, so the steady attendance re-
dounded to the credit of the lecturer especially, but also of his Italian
audience who have been able to follow a text that was not easy.

As Joyce indicated yesterday, he had purposely refrained from
critical or philosophical disquisitions about the play he was reading
and interpreting. His first task was to explain the words. His original
and slightly bizarre talent changed the nature of this commentary,
which might otherwise have been dry, into attractive 'causeries'.
The words, the manners, and the dress of the Elizabethans stirred
the lecturer to literary and historical recollections which proved of
keen interest to an audience which had been his for so many hours.

Yesterday evening, accepting the duty of closing such a work with a critical synthesis, he read (in English translation) the attack of Voltaire on *Hamlet*, and then, suddenly, the eulogy of the same work by Georg Brandes. We think that many in an audience that was capable of following these lectures will find themselves encouraged, as Joyce intended, to read other works of the great Englishman in the original.

Joyce was rewarded by his audience yesterday, at the end, with warm and prolonged applause which was certainly meant to invite him to repeat this novel and highly successful experiment of lecturing in English to an Italian audience.

p. 49
(*Thomas McGreevy recorded . . .*)   I am grateful to his sister for sending me this note by him.

p. 51
'*the tragic love-tie . . .*'   Georg Brandes, *William Shakespeare* (London, 1911), pp. 381–2.

p. 52
'*At a performance in the theatre . . .*'   Ellmann, *James Joyce*, pp. 450–1.

p. 54
the portrait of Mona Lisa   *Critical Writings*, p. 79.

p. 58
'*. . . a paralytic travesty of Shakespeare*'   William M. Schutte, *Joyce and Shakespeare* (New Haven, Conn., 1957), p. 145.

p. 59
'*a touch of the artist*'   Joyce was pleased when Jacques Mercanton praised Bloom for his artistic qualities, and he commented that these had been largely ignored (*Les Heures de James Joyce*, p. 13).

p. 63
'*Nothing exists but subjective states . . .*'   N. Kemp Smith in T. H. Greene, *General Introduction to Hume's 'Treatise'* (London, 1874), pp. 79–80.

p. 71
'*a deathsman of the soul*'   *Ulysses*, p. 187 (239); Stephen is applying to Shakespeare a word which Robert Greene uses in another context, presumably to fill out the epithet of 'a tiger's heart' which was in Greene's attack.

Chapter III JOYCE

p. 73
'*political . . . power of making the world*'   Roland Barthes, *Mythologies*, trans. Annette Lavers (Frogmore, 1973), p. 143.

p. 74
sincerity . . . the supreme virtue   Mercanton, *Les Heures de James Joyce*,
p. 17, and Padraic Colum, 'Portrait of James Joyce', *Dublin Maga-
zine*, Apr.–June 1932, p. 45.

p. 75
in no one . . . was the joy of life so keen   Stanislaus Joyce, *My Brother's
Keeper* (London and New York, 1958), p. 195.

conscience . . . meaning consciousness   Edward Engelberg, *The Unknown
Distance: from Consciousness to Conscience* (Cambridge, Mass., 1972).

p. 76
Homer's Ulysses wishes . . .   'I am, and my father was before me, a
violent Tory of the old school;—Walter Scott's school, that is to say,
and Homer's.' John Ruskin's opening sentence in *Praeterita*.

p. 77
indifference to politics   Lionel Trilling, *Beyond Culture* (New York,
1965), pp. 166–7.

failed . . . to display the evils of modern industrialism   S. L. Goldberg,
The Classical Temper (London, 1961), pp. 305–6.

p. 83
the bloodthirstiness of Church and State   See *Stephen Hero*, p. 190.

p. 89
Ireland was achieving independence . . .   Professor Patrick McCarthy
informs me that this theory is confirmed by Valery Larbaud, who
in a controversy over *Ulysses* with Ernest Boyd, pointed out not only
the parallel I had inferred but also an additional one, that Larbaud's
own lecture at the bookshop of Adrienne Monnier took place on 7
December 1921, the day of the armistice that followed the signing
of the treaty between England and the Irish representatives. See
Larbaud's reply in *Nouvelle revue française*, XXIV (Jan. 1925), pp. 5–
17, reprinted in his *Oeuvres complètes* (Paris, 1950–5), III. 401–16.
Joyce was in close touch with Larbaud in this controversy, and will
have cued him to specify these coincidences.

pp. 92–3
'*1) God's in his heaven . . . patriark alone*'   *Selected Letters of James Joyce*,
ed. Richard Ellmann (New York, 1975; London, 1976), p. 326.

p. 94
Such oversenses shape whole chapters   See Richard Ellmann, *Ulysses on
the Liffey* (London and New York, 1972), for fuller documentation
on this point.

Index

Aeolus (episode), 25–6, 81; Taylor's speech in, 34–8; J's adaptation from Homer, 40; Bloom and Stephen in, 68; J on newspapers, 78
aesthetics, J's theories, 9, 68–72; and politics, 73ff., 90–4
Agamemnon, 45
Aloysius, St., 55
anarchism, 82–6
Andreyev, Leonid, 7
anti-Semitism, 39, 41–2
Appel, Alfred, 137
Aquinas, Thomas, 7, 49
Argonautica, 45; Jason and Ulysses, 48
Aristophanes, 7
Aristotle, 7, 43, 94, 138; Bloom on, 39; on subjectivity, 63
Arnold, Matthew, 38
Artifoni, Almidano, 84
artist, J's conception of, 1, 48, 52, 55, 74–5; Stephen as, 20–1, 59; personal life of, 22; in *Circe*, 42; Hamlet as, 46; Shakespeare as, 50; revenge of, 53; Bloom as, 59; cerebral mating, 68–72; androgyny of, 69
Auden, W. H., 78–9
Auerbach, Erich, 38
Aurelius Antoninus, Marcus, 7

Bacon, Francis, on Daedalus, 18; on *Odyssey*, 28–9
Bakunin, Michael, 83–4
Balzac, Honoré de, J borrows motto from, 3, 4; books of, 7
Bandello, Matteo, 7
Barrie, J. M., 7

Barthes, Roland, 73
Beatrice (in *Exiles*), 49
Beaumont, Francis, 7
Beethoven, Ludwig van, 7
Bérard, Victor, on Semitic *Odyssey*, 27–9, 34
Bergson, Henri, 7
Berkeley, George, 7, 66
Björnson, Björnstjerne, 7
Blake, William, 7, 46
blood, 32
Bloom, Harold, 47–8
Bloom, Leopold, as salesman, 8; experiment with gulls, 8–9; calls Stephen by first name, 12; his pseudonym Henry, 21; and his father, 31; counterpointed with Stephen, 40–2; endangered, 42; and King Hamlet, 48; and Prince Hamlet, 47; relation to Mulvey and Gibraltar, 49; and madmen, 50; Freudian slip, 55; called 'Mr.', 60; and Shakespeare, 59–61, 68; cuckoldry of, 65; and selfhood, 67; as artist, 70–71; as statesman, 80–1, 83–6; and Bloomusalem, 85–6; and Griffith, 86–9; thoughts of food, 93–4; on closed system, 95
Bloom, Molly, 19; and Bloom's first name, 13; different aspects of, 30, 136; among rhododendrons, 41; joins Stephen and Bloom, 42; and Gibraltar, 49; and Anne Hathaway, 61; on politics, 86–8; solecism by, 92
Bloom, Rudy, 70

Boehme, Jacob, on signatures, 11
Bourget, Paul, 22
Boyd, Ernest, 141
Boylan, Blazes, and Trojan horse, 43, 58; and selfhood, 67
Boyle, William, 7
Bradley, A. C., 56
Brandes, Georg, 59; on Shakespeare and Goethe, 51
Breton, Nicholas, 59
Brontë, Charlotte, 7
Browning, Robert, 7
Bruno, Giordano, 7; as father of modern philosophy, 11
Budgen, Frank, 23, 135; on Homeric parallels, 24
Butler, Samuel, 7; on Homer, 23–4; as influence on J, 26–9; on metempsychosis, 92
Byron, May, on Shakespeare, 59–61

Callidike, 30
Carlyle, Thomas, 68
Carr, Henry, 17, 82, 83–4
Carthusians, motto of, 3
Catholicism, Joyce on, 1–2; see also Church
Cervantes, Miguel de, 7
Chamber Music, compound words in, 26
Chateaubriand, François-René de, 7
Childs, murder case, 45
Church, J's rebellion against, 1–2, 77; Stephen and Mulligan on, 20; J's attitude to, 49–50, 79–84, 90
Ciconians, 32
Circe (episode), 58; and Faust, 20; Bérard's view, 27; J's revision of Homer, 32, 40–1; Stephen in, 42; artistic engendering in, 42, 55, 70–1; Trojan horse in, 43; mirror in, 57–8; ghosts, 58–9; selfhood in, 63; time and space in, 66; doubling in, 91

Cixous, Hélène, 14
Clare, Maurice, see Byron, May
Coleridge, Samuel Taylor, on subjectivity in Homer, 44
Colum, Padraic, 7
Conrad, Joseph, 7, 15
Conmee, Revd. John S., 80–1
Connolly, Thomas E., catalogue of J's Paris library, 6, 98
consciousness, defined, 1
Constant, Benjamin, 7
countersense, 93
Countess Cathleen, The, J's support for, 2
Cyclops (episode), 19, 43, 73, 81; Zoilo-Thersites in Goethe, 21; anti-Semitism in, 41–2; selfhood in, 63, 67; chauvinism in, 87

Daedalus, preferred to Orpheus by J, 3; spelling first used by J, 12; use in A Portrait, 14–19; designs Trojan horse, 43; 'complex', 56
D'Annunzio, Gabriele, 7, 48
Dante Alighieri, 7; and exile, 4; and ricorso, 23, 26; use of vernacular, 26; his version of Ulysses, 29–30; Trojan horse in, 43; and Virgil, 48; J's use of, 49–50; and Shakespeare, 60; ultimate purpose of, 76
'Dead, The' (story), 87
Deasy, Garrett, 57, 58
Dedalus, Mrs., as ghost, 59, 70–1
Dedalus, Stephen, on imagination, 4; called by first name, 12; naming of, 14–19; mission of, 17; sense of humour, 18; danger of selfhood, 20; contempt for rhetoric, 38; counterpointed with Bloom, 40, 41, and Hamlet, 45–6, 51–2, 57; attitude to culture, 48; and Dante, 49; on madmen, 50; his two parables, 53; and Mallarmé, 62–3; and Dujardin,

64–5; his battle with time and space, 65–6; as artist, 70–1; on life, 74–5; as statesman, 80–1, 83–4; convergence with Bloom, 90–1

Defoe, Daniel, 7

De Valera, Eamon, 89

Dickens, Charles, 7

Disraeli, Benjamin, 7

Don Giovanni, list of lovers in, 29

'Dooleysprudence', 84–5

Dostoevsky, Fyodor, 7

doublet, Bérard's theory of, 27

doubt, 63

Dowland, John, songs of, 4

'Drama and Life', 48, 68

Dubliners, 15, 77, 88

Dujardin, Edouard, 7; as influence on J, 63–6

Earwicker, H. C., peccadilloes of, 45

Eliot, George, 7

Eliot, T. S., use of antiquity, 17; his Prufrock, 47; on time and space, 65

Engelberg, Edward, 75

Eugammon of Cyrene, his *Telegony*, 30

Exiles, Richard on nakedness, 1; source of plot, 22; Richard as woman-killer, 46; Beatrice in, 49; J's experiences in, 62; cuckoldry in, 64; and anarchism, 82

Ezekiel, 49

faith, Joyce's, 1

fatherhood, 52–4

Faust, and *Ulysses*, 19–21, 50–1; use of medieval world, 48–9

Fénelon, S., 31

Fielding, Henry, 7

Finnegans Wake, theory of art in, 3, 4; HCE and ALP in, 13; the symbolic E, 13–14; melting of myths in, 19; language of, 26; passage discussed, 92–3; oversense in, 94–5

Firbolgs, 33

FitzGerald, Edward, 7

Flaubert, Gustave, 7, 14, 64, 77; J's attitude to, 73

Fletcher, John, 7

Fogazzaro, Antonio, 7

France, Anatole, 7

Freud, Sigmund, on Leonardo, 54; on slips of tongue, 55; on unconscious, 55; J's use of, 56, and disagreement with, 56–57

fusion, of Bloom and Stephen, 40

Galsworthy, John, 7

Gerard, 60, 61

ghosts, in *Hamlet* and *Ulysses*, 52–59, 70–1

Giacomo Joyce, unnamed pupil in, 12

Gibraltar, 29–30

Gide, André, 7

Gilbert, Stuart, 20, 135; and Homeric parallels, 24

Gillet, Louis, discusses music with J, 4

Giraldus Cambrensis, 16

Gissing, George, 7

Gladstone, William Ewart, 2

Gluck, C. W., 7

God, 17; J on, 25, 50, 72

Godwin, William, 7

Goethe, Johann Wolfgang von, 7, 50; withholds last scene of *Faust*, 14; Wilhelm Meister's name, 15; *Faust* and *Ulysses*, 20–1, 50–1; use of medieval world, 48–9; *Wilhelm Meister* and *Hamlet*, 51–2

Gogarty, Oliver St. John, 61–2

Gogol, Nikolay, 7

Goldoni, Carlo, 7

Goldberg, S. L., 77–8

Goldsmith, Oliver, 7

Gorgonzola, 41

Gorky, Maxim, 7

'Grace' (story), sources of, 8

Greek, J's knowledge of, 24, 25–26; relation to Hebrew, 27

Greene, Robert, 140

Gregory, Augusta, Lady, 7; J's letter to, 1

Griffith, Arthur, J's early interest in, 55; Molly Bloom on, 86–7

Haines (in *Ulysses*), 20

Hamlet, 9; Stephen's theory of, 21, 56–7; Mulligan on, 21; parallel with Orestes, 45; and Telemachus, 46; relation to Stephen, 47, and to Bloom, 47; J's theory of, 48; J and Goethe on, 50–2, 62; two ghosts in, 52–9, Jones on, 56; Mallarmé on, 62–3; corruption in Denmark, 67; soliloquy in, 67; J's lectures on, 137–9

Hamsun, Knut, 7

Hardy, Barbara, 136

Hardy, Thomas, 7

Harte, Bret, 7

Hathaway, Anne, 53, 61

Hauptmann, Gerhart, 7; political aptitude, 76

Healy, Michael, sends books to J, 6

Hebrews, and *Odyssey*, 27; J's interest in Jews, 34; Taylor's Mosaic analogy, 34–8

Hegel, G. W. F., on epic, 39

Heijermans, Hermann, *Ahasver*, 34

Helen of Troy, 43

Herring, Phillip F., 136

history, 42

Homer, 7, 22; on Sirens, 4; on not naming hero, 12; and *ricorso*, 23; J's adaptation, 24–25; J's use of Homeric epithets, 25, and formulae, 25–6; Butler on, 26–7; Bérard on, 27–9; Tiresias' prophecy in, 29; J's changes in, 39–40, 42; gastronomy, 41; description of

Odysseus, 42; Telemachus in, 46; amalgamated with Shakespeare, 72; as Tory, 76

Hume, David, 7, 94; on subjectivity, 63

Huysmans, Joris-Karl, 7

Hyman, Louis, 39

Ibsen, Henrik, 7, 22, 55, 76; as J's example, 2; J's letter to, 3; J's reservations about, 10; *Peer Gynt* and *Ulysses*, 19–20; and Shakespeare, 50; womanliness of, 69

Icarus, 18–19

Iliad, 42

imagination, J's view of, 3–4, 65, 70–2; Vico on, 3

impersonality, J on, 3

internal monologue, 63–4

Ireland, brought to Continent by J, 7; and Greece, 10; as Ogygia, 23; and Palestine, 34–38, 81; as Hellas, 39; and fanaticism, 80; Bloom and Stephen on, 83–5; Free State and *Ulysses*, 88, 140

Ithaca, catechism in, 8

Jacobsen, J. P., 7

James, Henry, 7, 15

Jason, 48

Jews, *see* Hebrews and anti-Semitism

Joachim, Abbot, 50

Jones, Ernest, on *Hamlet*, 54, 56

Jolas, Eugene, 3

Joyce, Mrs. May (mother), unpersuaded by son, 2

Joyce, Nora, J's proselyte, 2–3; and J's putative cuckoldry, 22–3; calls J 'Woman-killer', 46; dream notebook of, 52–3

Joyce, Stanislaus, J's disciple, 2; J writes to about exile, 4, and Daedalus, 12; common frailty, 55; preserves J's library, 6; discusses psychology with J, 22

Jung, Carl Gustav, 54

Keller, Gottfried, 7
Kipling, Rudyard, 7
Kock, Paul de, 7, 64
Kropotkin, Peter, 82

Laertes, 51, 58, 62
landscape, and language, 5
language, versus music, 5; in *Finnegans Wake*, 26
Larbaud, Valery, 63, 141
Lawrence, D. H., 7, 77
Lee, Sidney, 59
Lenin, 17
Leopardi, Giacomo, 7
Lermontov, M. Y., 7
Le Sage, Alain René, 7
Lestrygonians (episode), structure of, 41, 68–9; attitude in, 75
Lewis, Wyndham, 7, 14
library, J's books in Trieste, 6–8, and Appendix
Linati, Carlo, J's scheme sent to, 30
Little Review, serializes *Ulysses*, 24
Litz, A. Walton, 138
Longfellow, Henry Wadsworth, 7
Loti, Pierre, 7
Lotus-Eaters (episode), J's modification of Homer in, 32
love, 41, 67

McCarthy, Patrick, 141
MacDowell, Gerty, 42, 51
McGreevy, Thomas, 49
Machiavelli, Nicolò, 7
Macnamara, Brinsley, 7
Macpherson, James, 7
Maeterlinck, Maurice, 7
Magrini, Gustavo, 7
Mallarmé, Stéphane, opposed by Yeats, 10, theory of *Hamlet*, 62–3
Mangan, James Clarence, poems set to music, 4; 'The Nameless One', 12; J's essay on, 75

Mangnall, Richmal, 8
Mann, Heinrich, 7
Marryat, Frederick, 7
Marx, Karl, 77, 78
Massinger, Philip, 7
masturbation, 7; and *Hamlet*, 21
Maupassant, Guy de, 7
Médecin de campagne, Le (Balzac), influence on J, 3
medieval world, 48
memory, related to imagination, 3, 4, 65, 70–2
'Memory of the Players at Midnight, A,' 47
Mephistopheles, and Mulligan, 20–1; song of, 51
Mercanton, Jacques, 25; on J's theory of imagination, 3; J comments about *Ulysses* to, 46
Meredith, George, use of *Odyssey*, 10, 31
Mérimée, Prosper, 7
metempsychosis, 91–2
micturition, J has book on, 8
Milton, John, 7; history of man in, 29
Mirbeau, Octave, 7
Molière, 7
moly, 42
Mona Lisa, 54
Moore, George, 7
Morris, William, 75
Moses, 35–9, 80
Mozart, W. A., 7; *Don Giovanni*, 29
Mulligan, Buck, and Mephistopheles, 20–1; anti-Semitism of, 39; and Trojan horse, 43; as usurper, 58; and selfhood, 67; materialism of, 83
Murray, Mrs. Josephine, 24
music, J's attitude to, 4–5; J's manual of, 7–8; and literature, 75

Nabokov, Vladimir, J on Homeric parallels to, 24, 137
Nausicaa (episode), 73, 138; J's

and Homer's compared, 33; Gerty MacDowell in, 42, 51
Nazism, J's antipathy to, 89–90
Nelson, Admiral Horatio, 81
Nietzsche, Friedrich, 7
Nothung, 55, 66

Odysseus, Homer's puns on name, 13; J's etymology of, 13; Butler on, 25–6, 28–9; Bérard on, 26–9; Bloom's counterpoint with, 42; in Dante, 49; in Shakespeare, 76
Odyssey, 9, 45, 52; new *Odyssey* predicted by Yeats, 11, and attempted by J, 11; as allegory, 24–5; relation to *Ulysses*, 30–1, 47, 58; murder case in, 45; usurpation theme, 58; gods in, 65
Oedipus complex, 56; repudiated by J, 57
O'Flaherty, Roderic, on Ogygia, 23
Ogygia, Calypso's isle and Ireland, 23
O'Kelly, Seamas, 7, 76
Ophelia, 46, 50, 51, 62, 67
Ordish, T. F., 61
Orestes, 45–6, 53, 57
oversense, 94–5
Ovid, on Ulysses, 13, on Daedalus, 18
Oxen of the Sun (episode), source of parodies in, 8; artistic and natural creation in, 69

Palmer, Mrs. Bandman, 47
Paolieri, Ferdinando, 7
Parnell, Charles Stewart, Joyce's view of, 2, 80, 86, 88
Patrick, St., 14, and Ulysses, 33
Peer Gynt, and *Ulysses*, 19–20
Penelope, 73, 74; Bacon on, 29; and Gertrude, 46; and bed, 58
Petrarch, 74
Phoenicians, and *Odyssey*, 27
Plutarch, on Greek E at Delphi,

13–14; calls Ireland Ogygia, 23
Poe, Edgar Allan, 7
politics, 73ff.
Polti, Georges, 48
'Portrait of the Artist', A', first draft of novel, 2; unnamed hero in, 12, 15; politics in, 77–78
Portrait of the Artist as a Young Man, A, exile in, 4; villanelle, 5; Yeats in, 10; naming of hero, 11–12, 14–19; extrapolated in *Ulysses*, 19, 25; Stephen's mission, 20–1; and Vico, 23; compound words in, 26; kept separate from *Ulysses*, 32; muse on strand in, 42; culture in, 48; sexual jealousy in, 57; spiritual and physical birth in, 71–2; peroration, 74–5; Church in, 77; social regeneration theme, 79; nationalism, 84
Pound, Ezra, on artistic creation, 5; on parallels with *Odyssey*, 23
Power, Arthur, 138
Praga, Marco, 7
Proteus (episode), external world in, 63; spiritual progress in, 64; on space and time, 65–6
Proudhon, P. J., 82–3
pun, 90–4; as Joycean key, 90–1; on names and personages, 90–91

Rabelais, François, 7
Radek, Karl, 77
Renard, Jules, 7
Renan, Ernest, 55
Reynolds, Mary T., 49
Rich, Penelope, 47
Richards, Grant, 88
Rooney, William, 87
Roscher, W. N., 13
Ruskin, John, 141
Russell, Bertrand, 7

Russell, George, 67; etherealism, 83

Sacher-Masoch, Leopold von, 7
Schopenhauer, Arthur, 7
Schutte, William M., on J's reading, 59
Scott, Sir Walter, 7
Scylla and Charybdis (episode), theory of art in, 21, 52–3; in *A Portrait*, 25; Bacon's view of, 29; structure of, 41, 68–9; external world in, 63
sea shore, 8
sexuality, J's view of, 2, 55
Shakespeare, Hamnet, 53, 57
Shakespeare, William, 7; Stephen's view of, 50–1; compared with Bloom, 57; see also *Hamlet*
Shaun, 3
Shaw, Bernard, 7
Sheehy-Skeffington, Francis, 55
Shelley, Percy Bysshe, 55; on imagination, 4
Shem, as artist, 3
Siegfried, 55, 66
sin, J's view of, 2
Sinn Féin, 86–8
Sirens (episode), Ulysses and, 5; music in, 8; structure, 41; Gerard in, 61; and art, 75
'Sisters, The' (story), malapropisms in, 55
Smidt, Kristian, 137
Smollett, Tobias, 7
socialism, J relates to art, 1; J's brand of, 78–9, 94–5; books on, 82
Stanford, W. B., 31, 136
state (British), J's opposition to, 2, 77–84, 90; Stephen and Mulligan on, 20
Stephen Hero, title of, 15; Dante in, 49; artist in, 69; affirmation in, 75; and 'new humanity', 79
Sterne, Laurence, 7

Stoppard, Tom, 17
Strindberg, August, 7
Sue, Eugène, 34
Svevo, Italo, 7, 54
Swift, Jonathan, 7, 50
Synge, John Millington, 7

Taylor, John F., speech of, 34–8
Telemachus, 138; in *Odyssey* and *Ulysses*, 24, 39–40, 46, 51; in Fénelon, 31; and *Telegony*, 30; and suitors, 58
Thersites, 21, 67
Thoth, 17
time and space, 53; discussed, 65–8; related to Church and State, 79–82; as oversense, 74
Tiresias, prophesies Ulysses' last voyage, 29–30
Tolstoy, Leo, 7; J's admiration for, 74
Trilling, Lionel, 77
Trojan horse, used in *Ulysses*, 42–3; describes *Ulysses* itself, 79
Tucker, Benjamin, 83
Turgenev, Ivan, 7
Twain, Mark, 34
Tysdahl, B. J., 136
Tzara, Tristan, 17

undersense, 90–4

Vallancey, Charles, on Irish as Phoenicians, 34
Vaughan, Revd. Bernard, 55
Vico, Giambattista, on imagination and memory, 3; on *ricorso* in Homer and Dante, 23; and Bacon, 28–9; on Homer's not being delicate, 39
Virgil, 7; and tradition, 10; on not naming hero, 12; follows Homer, 31, 42, 45, 48; and *Argonautica*, 45
Voltaire, 50

Wagner, Richard, 7; *Flying Dutchman*, 34; Siegfried, 55

Wallace, Charles William, 59
Wandering Rocks (episode), 41,
  81
Weaver, Harriet Shaw, 69
Wedekind, Frank, 7
Weiss, Edoardo, 54
Wells, H. G., 7
Whitman, Walt, 95
Wilde, Oscar, 17; and new Hel-
  lenism, 39
Wilhelm Meister, 51–2, 62
Wilson, J. Dover, 59
Wood, J. C., 8

Woolf, Virginia, 7
Wordsworth, William, 31–2

Yeats, William Butler, 7, 15, 74,
  75; poems sung by J, 4; re-
  buked by Stephen, 10; and
  tradition, 10, 48; predicts new
  Odyssey, 10–11; and masks, 16;
  song in *Countess Cathleen*, 20;
  ethics in, 50; symbology, 68

Zoilus, 21
Zola, Emile, 7